Fifty Years to Say
I Love You

Hope for Broken Relationships Healing
from Trauma & Passages to Recovery

TaJuana J. Davis

WESTBOW°
P R E S S
A DIVISION OF THOMAS NELSON
& ZONDERVAN

Scriptures taken from the Holy Bible, New International Version®, NIV®. Copyright © 1973, 1978, 1984, 2011 by Biblica, Inc.™ Used by permission of Zondervan. All rights reserved worldwide. www.zondervan.com The "NIV" and "New International Version" are trademarks registered in the United States Patent and Trademark Office by Biblica, Inc.™ All rights reserved.

WestBow Press books may be ordered through booksellers or by contacting:

WestBow Press
A Division of Thomas Nelson & Zondervan
1663 Liberty Drive
Bloomington, IN 47403
www.westbowpress.com
1 (866) 928-1240

Because of the dynamic nature of the Internet, any web addresses or links contained in this book may have changed since publication and may no longer be valid. The views expressed in this work are solely those of the author and do not necessarily reflect the views of the publisher, and the publisher hereby disclaims any responsibility for them.

Any people depicted in stock imagery provided by Thinkstock are models, and such images are being used for illustrative purposes only. Certain stock imagery © Thinkstock.

ISBN: 978-1-4908-4763-4 (sc)
ISBN: 978-1-4908-4764-1 (hc)
ISBN: 978-1-4908-4762-7 (e)

Library of Congress Control Number: 2014914459

Printed in the United States of America.

WestBow Press rev. date: 08/25/2014

Biblical truths! Empowered courage! Healing and recovery!....I recommend this book to anyone searching for freedom from the chains of trauma.

- Mark Gregston, Heartlight Radio/Dealing with Today's Teens Ministries.

TaJuana's non-judgmental approach taught me to open my heart, discover self-respect, and embrace HEALING! A huge heart for God!!
- (T. F. client)

TaJuana helped me in so many ways. I now have a more positive outlook on my life, gained healthier coping skills, and no longer turning to destructive choices when trauma from my past resurfaces....

Zhanna – client

> **I cried out to the Lord and He answered by setting me free – Psalm 118:4**

CONTENTS

PREFACE

You are about to walk through pages etched in passages that unfold into a life of heart-changing journeys for hope - fifty years of discovering healing.

As I share what inspired me to begin my journey for truth, my hope is that you will allow the following passages to become a divine inspiration moving you toward discovering the key that will unlock your own chapters of truth. This great discovery can guide you in finding your own journey to healing and recovery. It may be that you have been stuck in emotional secrets that could add truth to your personal journey, if the ability to unlock those secrets were ever revealed to you. Perhaps you have even finally found the desire to take ownership of your brokenness caused by the pain from your past and now asking, "What do I do with this discovery?"

I know too well of the pain and confusion that accompanies a home filled with brokenness caused from anger and hostility. At an early age I witnessed how this environment paved the way to acts of unhealthy, as well as unsafe, circumstances which later led to trust issues with others and much doubt within myself. For years I didn't understand the damage I had endured from the exposure to these un-invited circumstances during my childhood.

Later in my life the reality of my injuries began to surface and so did the awareness of how strongly these injuries impacted me emotionally. It was at that point I began to understand that if I didn't take charge and find a way to free myself from the strong hold of the chains from my past, my life would be consumed by these memories and remain stuck in their bondage.

I refused to allow the past to determine my future!

As I began fighting for the freedom for healing and recovery I found support from others to be huge! But more importantly what I discovered is if I'm not turning to solid support when in need of guidance, then the situations which I desire to escape from can become most destructive. I am so grateful to many who have walked along-side me while offering wise counsel. I need to begin here by sharing my deep appreciation to a very special friend God brought into my life for only a short while named Jackie Hodge, who inspired me to write this book. She supported me with solid direction through her transparency about her own journey to recovery which encouraged me to move from what was once only my vision, to a message of purpose. A purpose that is now being "lived out loud" in the lives of those who choose to journey with me in these rock solid passages to recovery.

The realization of needing to share what I had once become fond of calling "my story" was not evident until Jackie sat down with me and told me she thought I should write a book. As simple as that! Like many, I had never had any thoughts, let alone confidence, in having anything worthwhile to share that others would not have already figured out through their own battles. As our conversation continued I found myself being quite confused about her belief in my ability to take on such an endeavor. I initially found it to be nothing more than an unrealistic idea. I later discovered that the reasons for having no confidence that my story would hold any significance to others mirrors the same reasons that led me to a clearer vision in needing to share it even more.

Many have a story, but not all will come to a safe place of recognizing the purpose or meaning that lies within the struggles of their life story, therefore keeping it to themselves. This recognition can be a powerful tool toward the starting line for the race to a journey of truth that can finally lead us to healing. But this initial step to healing can also come with a great amount of weight when discovering that this same starting line puts us on the frontline of becoming transparent about the pain in our past; our secrets are now exposed! This discovery can be somewhat paralyzing causing many to drop out of their race before finding truth for healing. Preparing our hearts for this journey-- which this book will equip you to do--is a critical piece in staying the course when the realities of what brought us to need healing begin to take shape.

The reality for me was discovering that my exposure to constant rage, hostile fits, and withholding of love was in truth acts of verbal, emotional abuse, and physical abuse. During the many years I spent denying the truth about abuse that took place brought to me a false sense of reality. I now acknowledge that this denial was a necessary coping mechanism there to protect me from what I was not ready to accept about those truths at that time. Still, the losses that developed during those years robbed me of joy with what should have been my most meaningful and closest relationships that could have grown more intimate if having the adequate tools to nurture them the way I was created to.

Once I gave into naming the injuries from my past, God began revealing to me the many flaws which I had so idealistically convinced myself were absent in my life. One of the many discoveries I made while on this journey to truth was that abuse creates a need of perfection to it's victims in order for us to control what we could not be controlled during the years the abuse took place. I was not exempt from this!

No matter how hard I tried, I was forced to realize that a life of perfection was not in my reach!

Learning to be transparent--there is nothing neither easy nor pleasant about it! But then I discovered there is much freedom in the truths that drive us to live our lives out loud in the way we were created to--and when being truthful with myself, in the way I most desired. Still, it didn't come without *much* hard work. A tremendous barrier of self-doubt often surrounded me when feeling drawn to act out my faith that would bring me closer to living my life out loud in the way I was created.

Beneath the hard work that brought me through the tough steps of healing, I found that God's word would replace my self-doubt and eventually move me to begin speaking about the intimate truths that would later lead others in knowing they too can have a place and time of healing.

> ### *The voice of the Lord is powerful, Psalm 29:4!!*

No matter how huge the barriers, I now know they are very capable of being removed if the desire is there. A break through to freedom from the past pain is a great discovery.

My hope is that while spending time going through these chapters, you too will be empowered to act out your faith where it has become weakened with doubt. The message you will be searching for is not in my story itself, but a message knitted together from personal journeys of others, that will not have to end when yours begin.

ABOUT THE AUTHOR

TaJuana is a licensed social worker and holds a diploma in Professional Christian Life Coaching. She is president, director, and founder of Living Hope Ministries, Inc. providing coaching and counsel to individuals and families in crisis situations involving pregnancies, parenting, along with marriage and family relationships; including assisting with intense needs such as domestic violence, abuse, and anger alternatives.

TaJuana works alongside her husband Terry, an ordained minister, in ministry and local and international missions. They have been married 31 years and have three adult children Trace and wife Kara, Taryn, and Charles-Taylen. They reside in Princeton, Ky. TaJuana is available for speaking engagements for church groups, conferences, and offers workshops on a variety of topics concerning family issues.

She can be contacted at www.livinghopeministriesky.com or 270-625-5926.

SPECIAL ACKNOWLEDGEMENTS

I have found truth in this phrase, "GOD IS SOOOOO GOOD"!

If you don't believe this you have not "yet" opened your eyes to His great love, mercy and grace I am about to unapologetically share. I pray that this book will lead you to also believing in this truth, and that you will allow this belief to walk you through the following "Passages to Recovery."

I praise God for my always patient and loving helpmate, Terry. His love for Jesus can not be measured and after 31 years I have finally figured out that his love for me can not be measured either. I am so proud to be the mother to our children--Trace and wife Kara, Taryn, and Bo, which our creator so carefully and selflessly hand selected for us. Much thanks to each of you for always being a patient listener when asking for your advice for this book, and for your patience with me during the many days of hibernating while compiling these pages.

I am especially grateful to my parents for giving me a love for life, and with God's grace, a heart for serving others. To my parents, Charles and Pat, I love you and owe you both much thanks for giving me the opportunity to take a stand on truths that I have witnessed each of you take, though in your own way and through your own unique journey. The discoveries you have made in your journey will not end with you but will continue through the lives which were shaped through your ongoing contributions.

THANK YOU

Cec Murphy, Chad Oliver, Debbie Scott, George Stahnke, Jackie Hodge, Drew Hudgins, Mark Gregston, Olivia Boaz, Ron and Rodetta Cook, Bro Ronnie Sivells, family and friends who encouraged me through the completion of this book, and to the many clients I am privileged to walk alongside who adds much value and strength to this book.

GUARDING YOUR HEART

Determining the difference between the story behind our life and a journey through our life is a valuable part of guarding your heart from the deep rooted discoveries waiting to unfold. When we realize that we don't have to own every piece of thread that's been knitted into our lives, the two can more easily be separated. Some things are rooted so deeply that it's difficult to name what it is we are holding onto--and then some are things that never should have been ours to hold. The inability to be released from what doesn't belong to us can create a silence in our lives that secretly replaces the very purpose we are in constant search for, making it easier for many to find it more comforting to remain stuck in the story behind their life --or in other words, to remain stuck in their past.

Acceptance of what we have been handed in life doesn't always come easy. When reality hits that remaining stuck in the past is what we've allowed to define our lives--finding freedom (if only an ounce at a time) to let go of the stories that hold no positive influence for our future can more easily become our reality. Learning to let go of the pieces in our life's story is the beginning steps to a beautiful journey of healing and recovery.

Determining the difference between my story and my journey was key for me. After much thought, I have come up with my own definition to separate the two. Both are intended to help set the stage for what I hope will move you forward in your personal steps toward healing and recovery.

Stories can be fabricated and shaped into what we want for ourselves, and particularly others, to see or believe in order to disguise what we don't want to exist. Our perception becomes our coping mechanism. Journeys take time and effort, and in a sense, take on a physical appearance of undeniable genuineness that can actually be seen and touched by others when living our journey out loud in sincere truth and purpose. Opposite from the self-created stories, we are now taking on a newly formed presence that can't be disguised. Once I found the courage to examine my perceived reality, I also found freedom from the need to disguise the truth which I had created for my own purposes of guarding my heart from what I didn't want to know existed.

Take the time now to reflect on how you might begin moving toward a personal journey to healing and recovery that no longer has to be explained to yourself or anyone else, just lived out loud in truth as you simply keep walking through that journey of faith. Faith isn't always seen, but when experienced the feeling is very real. So real that you keep on doing what you're doing because you know there is something more with each step ahead, with no concern for the reasons behind the steps of faith you continue to take--no looking back.

1. Do you find yourself holding onto things that you should have never been yours to own?

2. What pieces of threads knitted into your life are you ready to be separated from?

3. From what are you guarding your heart?

4. Are you ready to begin that journey that will give you freedom to live your life out loud in truth and no more masks to hide behind?

These and other questions will be unveiled as you begin to live your life out loud through your journey of truths and purpose.

PREPARING FOR THE JOURNEY

Each chapter is designed to carry you from the beginning to the end of what will become your unique journey. In order to do so more effectively I first encourage you to read through the chapters in the order they are written. Then, participating in the self assessments will be helpful in pulling out any thoughts, feelings, and desires that motivate you to want to continue letting your story move you through the paths to your journey. I trust you will find these assessments helpful in moving you forward in your search to living your life in truth, as it was uniquely created to be lived out loud.

Set goals to search for understanding as you continue to read through each chapter that follows. You will notice similar statements or questions being repeated throughout the chapters. This was done for purposes of stretching your thought processes to a deeper level than when first being confronted with the same past issues in the chapters you just read. Doing so will give you the greatest opportunity for the discovery of truths that will lead you to recovery, if allowing yourself to be completely honest with your answers. I know, too well, how easy it is to try and hide those truths even from myself. Again, that is a part of our coping mechanism.

This is a place you can let your guard down and focus on your most inner thoughts and needs and not be concerned about how your words may affect others' needs from being met, as you were likely accustom to practicing in the past. You are free to answer them according to your exact thoughts at that very moment. Regardless of what you answered in the previous chapters questions, and particularly regardless of how you would want to be viewed if others were allowed to read your most inner thoughts, write it as it is. Prepare yourself now to set boundaries around any obstacles that can interfere with being honest about who you are and what you hope to accomplish while spending time in these passages. You are worth the truth!

Depending on your circumstances, some of the questions in the assessments which you are asked to reflect on may be difficult to answer; especially if it is the first time you have been asked to share your feelings and thoughts surrounding deep rooted circumstances that cause old pain to surface. It is natural to want to shut down and not want to move any further in search for recovery at the first hint of discomfort. When you encounter these emotions, don't allow yourself to fall into the crippling effects that can cause this to happen. Rather, give yourself permission to take the time necessary to reflect on any uncomfortable emotions which these healing truths will begin to draw out.

Everyone hits a moment of truth! A section is provided at the end of each chapter titled "Journey Notes". When you come to a question which causes you to hit a moment of truth that you are not yet ready to walk through, turn to the "Journey Notes" write down the chapter and number for that question. Periodically, look through these notes to see what areas are keeping you stuck and when ready to continue traveling, return to that question and attempt to answer. You will discover throughout this book, how valuable the truth is. Please don't hesitate to take all the time you need in honestly answering these questions.

There is something extremely powerful in watching your thoughts come to life on paper, not to mention much safer than revealing the details to another person, at least until you are ready to trust how well it might be received by others. The more you learn about yourself, the stronger you will be in living out your life's intended purpose in truth.

Please take the time to look at the "Rock Solid Resource" section at the end of this book. These can be valuable resources at your finger tips for either yourself, or when walking alongside someone else who may be in need of your counsel.

I dedicate this journey to my father who left us to be with Jesus just before the completion of this book. And also to my mother-- known to many as Mamaw Crayne-- who remained obedient to her role of a most loving helpmate and personal prayer warrior to him, for 54 years. She continues to be a great role model to many today!

CHAPTER 1

SEARCH FOR TRUTH

"Why do I do the things I do?" "Why is this particular trait so ingrained in me that I can't seem to escape its grip, even when I desperately want to?" "Why am I so intensely emotional about a particular thing and at the same time I can never explain these emotions to anyone?" "What is the hard drive that's wired within that makes me feel so secure at one moment and so very insecure at another?"

These questions have not purposely been on my agenda to sort out; instead they developed slowly as life continued to happen in ways that were least uncomfortable for me. And for that matter, it's not been too many years now that I 've considered confronting these questions for fear of what I would discover once I began that journey of searching for answers. I believe there are plenty of people who at some point in their life began asking themselves "Who am I?" At the point I literally began asking myself this question, I quickly realized I didn't really want to know what I had not known for so many years. Through a lot of work I have since found the answers to be valuable learning tools. These learning tools would later bring strength to the future which I was created to live out loud. Yet I had fought so hard for so many years, refusing to believe this person within me, whom I thought I knew so well, could be someone so completely different.

Maybe this is where you are now - meeting that person who has shared your identity before ever conceived in your mother's womb, face-to-face for the very first time. I don't know about you, but I didn't handle this reunion as well as I would have wanted. I now know that I am not alone in this search for what I refer to as, "becoming the person I was created to be." While giving you a glimpse of what took place at an early age that structured my false awareness of who I was created to be, I can now confidently say that after fifty years of walking through the passages within these pages, I 've learned to live my life out loud in truth.

My prayer is that the following pages can guide you to the reality of how you too can live the life you were created to live with no apologies or explanations necessary.

Many adults spend years wanting to break free from the repeated cycle of patterns that continue to bring destruction in their lives. These destructive patterns can be so subtle that no one may ever know they exist and can even go unnoticed by the very person who is unfortunate enough to possess them. Life certainly does happen at the most inconvenient times. What was once known as a fairly normal and stable life can suddenly, and with no warning, become emotionally turned upside down. Then the silent search begins.

Some who experience these destructive patterns will choose to keep this out-of-sight, out-of-mind belief for a life time. Others learn the value of what has been discovered about themselves through these unpleasant experiences; a turning point that unfolds a strong realization that a missing link in their life—-though a not so pleasant discovery--has now been found. The discovery of the missing link is a valuable key to your recovery

While visiting these memories, preparing our heart for what has been kept under lock and key for so many years is a critical step. Begin by discovering the truth in who you really are, as well as what you are capable of doing with this new discovery that selflessly wants to illuminate your awareness of what has been locked away. The key to this missing link holds much power. Therefore, our approach in finding the right key that can effectively unlock these memories must be a cautious one, or we risk stirring up a vicious storm during our escape from the too familiar patterns that falsely bring us comfort. When past or present obstacles vie for control over your life, begin searching for real comfort in who you were created to be regardless of the lies in your present circumstances convincing you what you are to be. With practice, this will help soften the impact of the many stages of confusion that come along when breaking away from old patterns of false beliefs you once had about your self worth.

Do you ever find yourself desperately in search for answers in the midst of the largest of life's storms, only to discover in your busyness of "fixing things" the answers were actually right in front of you all along? I've found this to be typical for most of us—we are so busy solving our problems that we overlook the solution as one that will positively shape our future.

How often do we see the challenges in our life storms as a natural strengthening tool that if allowed can be beneficial in helping us cope with future challenges that will inevitably come our way? Few would disagree that the feeling of security is more easily found when life appears normal—when all is well. But when life gets turned upside down our tendencies are to cope by using the same old tools we have grown so accustomed to using: back to our old ways of trying to fix things with no positive outcome. When failing to grasp the answers that would have helped avoid destruction from the next storm before it hits, we continue to repeat the same old cycle that lead us to its destruction. Practicing these old ways will leave us with little opportunity to be still, embrace, and be strengthened by the quiet moments that will direct us toward the path of solid answers for which our hearts are really searching.

I want to stop here to validate that because I understand the reality of extreme difficulties some may have faced at one time or another, it may not seem appropriate to say our lives' storms can benefit us, when these storms may have brought on more pain than anyone deserves. I don't want to minimize the intensity of your circumstances, that for all the obvious reasons, you may find them much easier to deal with when not dealing with them at all. Rather, I hope to come alongside you, as others have unselfishly done for me, to guide you in discovering the unique tools God has equipped you with in navigating through these storms.

Each of us holds the ability to journey through rock solid passages that will lead to recovery and healing from destruction of past pain. Giving ourselves permission to take that journey is a huge step in breaking free from these repeated cycles of destructiveness that keep us in a false zone of comfort.

1. What are some characteristic traits which you find yourself asking, "Why do I do that?"

2. Do you find yourself spinning your wheels in constant need to "fix things" in yours or someone else's life with no resolution?

3. Do you have a need to be in control of everything around you? Give an example--

4. Have there been negative circumstances in your life that later you realized made you stronger? Give an example--

Journey Notes

CHAPTER 2

PIECES OF A STORY OPEN PASSAGES TO A JOURNEY

The more challenges I've experienced in life the greater the possibility to undeniably understand truth in the meaning of patience and trust. I cherish the lessons that have opened my heart to knowing such great value in these two attributes. The following are pieces of my story that have opened the door to this valuable discovery, and when the season was right, took me through passages to my journey that for much of my life I had unknowingly been in search for--at least, not until a time of continuous struggles that seemingly had no end. My recognition for healing and recovery from my past began to develop as a result of unhealthy coping skills during this time.

I want to walk you through the opening passages that began to highlight the severity of my struggles and ultimately started me on the path to a journey that brought me to the place of healing I know today.

We rarely prepare for anything to go wrong when planning for a weekend getaway. Everything seemed to fall into place when my husband Terry and I picked up our two younger children, Taryn and Bo, from school to kick off their fall break. Our suitcases were packed, in the car, and ready to hit the road when we pulled out of the schools parking lot. We decided to make one last stop at the local pizza place where our oldest son Trace worked, to tell him good-bye before we headed out to Louisville for the three day pastoral conference. We asked Trace one more time if he would reconsider and go with us. The original plans were for all three of our children to take the weekend trip as a family. Being middle school age, Taryn and Bo were excited about taking a day off from school and being away for the long weekend. Trace on the other hand was in his first year of community college and much more enthused about the rare occasion of having the weekend to himself. Knowing he would be staying with his grandmother brought us comfort, so we put trust in his last words "I'll be okay", and we pulled out of the parking lot for a weekend of fellowship with other pastors and their families.

When we returned home late on Saturday night I was curious about why my brother-in-law's truck was parked in our driveway. As he and his wife got out of their truck to meet us at our car, I wasn't prepared to be greeted with the news that Trace had been in a horrific car wreck. While questions rushed through my mind about how to trust that our son would be okay, they ended when hearing, "He is in the hospital and his friend did not survive". There are no words to describe the emotions of that moment--Trace being without us while enduring this most traumatic time in his life, our two younger children who we had 'not been able to prepare for this heart wrenching news, and the other parents who was suffering in the loss of their son--I instantly became overwhelmingly numb. The reality that was too difficult for me to grasp at that moment turned out to be more than real!

When we arrived at the hospital we learned that Trace had already gone through a series of surgeries. Doctors were not sure at this point how much the injuries would impact his future but were becoming more certain that his life was not at risk. Over a period of weeks being closely watched by hospital staff and with many efforts in a long term physical therapy program, Trace was eventually discharged to come home. After a couple more months of physical therapy, Trace could leave his wheelchair behind and rely only on the use of a cane for just a short while. It seemed as if he would recover reasonably well, the doctors called him a miracle!

Over a 1 1/2 year period after our son's wreck, he had undergone more surgeries and was preparing to move on with his life. His surgeon's only instructions were that he considers a career choice that required little physical labor, due to his lack of mobility. We were told he would also face early onset of arthritis, due to the severity of injuries to multiple bones throughout his body. Though we did not want to be insensitive about the reality of how these injuries would affect Trace and his future, my husband and I were both viewed this as a somewhat reasonable challenge--we had *not* lost our son!

As parents, we should have understood that survivor's guilt would leave him with great emotional needs which we would have no comprehension in how to provide care for. Doing the best we can do is not always doing enough! I now know that as parents we didn't recognize the extent of his needs and therefore couldn't comprehend the road this event would later take him down.

Trauma is not picky about who it chooses to bring suffering to. The years our children had known as a somewhat stress free, predictable environment that seemingly brought them much content and joy, quickly got turned upside down. I found I was far from an expert at keeping a healthy balance between meeting the needs of our two younger children and at the same time the needs of our son Trace, whose suffering was steadily growing without our knowledge. We later learned that survivor's guilt would leave him as a victim for PTSD (post traumatic stress syndrome). The heavy weight from this diagnosis required a seven month intensive therapeutic care facility which we found two thousand miles from home, and also led to several years of an intense recovery process once he returned home from receiving this care. The energy put into providing for his care was constantly pulling at my hearts strings on whether or not I was giving an adequate amount of quality and quantity time to both him, our two younger children and my marriage. Time will eventually tell you what you don't want to know.

Just six months prior to our family's life changing event, we received a phone call that my father-in-law's truck had flipped and was life flighted to Owensboro's brain trauma unit with no certainties he would survive the weekend. Only a few months later he was transported to a nursing facility in our home town with severe injuries that was too great for my husband's mother to care for at home. Many adjustments would be made in both the family and with the family's business as they prepared for the unknown. There was little hope that my father-in-law would ever regain mobility or speech, his head trauma was severe. Dealing with the emotions of this, along with our son's injuries from the wreck just a few months later, brought about many questions--the greatest being, "God, what else do you want from us"?

Trauma does not exempt anyone. It doesn't matter how much money you have, nor how little. It doesn't matter if you are young or old. And in our own personal experience, we quickly discovered that trauma is stingy enough to not care if you are in your prime years of wanting to shape many positive memories for your young children's future. No one is exempt from the impact of trauma.

Life happens at the most inconvenient times--we can never prepare for times such as these! Even when we'd seen first hand what real life experiences looked like, it would never seem possible there could be room for more.

As I go back to earlier years I am reminded of a time when our children were only 4, 5, and 10 years old when I got the call that my husband was at the emergency room. I quickly took our children across the street to our neighbor and left for the hospital. When I arrived the nurses were trying to stabilize him enough to be transported to a larger hospital that was equipped to care for stroke victims.

Early the next morning I went to visit my husband in ICU and in hopes I would catch the doctors before they left for their rounds. I wasn't prepared for his doctor's bedside manners. "He might as well have put a gun to his head, the pressure on his brain was so high that there is no guarantee he will have sight. I can't promise you what the outcome will be", were the only words this doctor spoke about my husbands condition before he turned and walked away. He left me feeling lost and alone.

After months of doctor's care and home rest, Terry was able to return to work. Strong warnings of required medical treatments were enforced in order to live a somewhat healthy life, even though a constant struggle of health issues continues to consume his life to this day. This early experience with trauma had not prepared me for what was to come throughout the next 18 years of challenges. We can't always pick and choose when we will allow interferences to enter our perfect world we think it should be.

The years to come were lined up with doctor and hospital visits, surgical procedures, and many uncertainties for Terry. There have been many days on end we could not predict his level of functioning. Although at times, the weight of this load put me in a role of playing a single parent raising three children, it was not until we faced our son's suffering that I began knowing I needed more strength than what I could ever provide on my own.

Being a pastor's wife, I felt I was supposed to be viewed as strong at handling things for our family, regardless of what I felt inwardly. That was one of the many mistakes I made while trying to sort through this massive time of confusion. I quickly discovered that pastoral families were not exempt from the impacts this world has to offer (we tend to view ourselves as living in glass walls and need to appear as close to perfect as possible--more misconceptions). I was forced to hit a moment of truth, trauma does not exempt anyone. Especially not me!

Fast forwarding in time when I realized I wasn't the "Super Woman" I had so falsely set myself up to be, I also began witnessing my own emotional well being spinning out of control. Severe panic attacks sent me to the emergency room more than once for an echo-cardiogram. As time continued I discovered that the impact of recent traumatic life events had triggered memories of trauma from earler years in my life which I thought had been packaged safely away in an out-of-sight, out-of-mind compartment. I had never intended for these thoughts to become unlocked. As these childhood memories continued to surface, so did my awareness that I could quickly lose control of my family I deeply cherished unless I choose to confront it with truth. It took years of repeated attempts of self efforts trying to fix what I was not equipped to fix on my own that only failed and at times ended with near destructive outcomes. There would be many bitter pills to swallow before I discovered the truth that would set me free!

In 2011, my husband Terry's heart gave him a sudden warning that led him straight to the hospital before we made it home from a weekend of what was to be a time for relaxation. Within a few weeks he was scheduled for a triple by-pass that later resulted in several trips in and out of the hospital over the next three months, due to complications from the surgery. The following year, while continuing his battle for recovery, Terry's father died, after ten years of nursing home care. That same year, my father died just six months later.

Throughout these years there were times that I felt I could not possibly take anymore heartache. There were times that I felt like giving up. There were even times that I felt God did not care enough about me to provide protection for me and my family from these heavy things that continued to control our lives. The realization of taking steps to talk to God about my anger that had been swelling up inside me through these decades of continuous heartache became evident, to my surprise He began talking back. An even greater surprise was His unexpected communication revealing to me small details of my painful childhood that I had never intended to visit.

Little by little, as the details got heavier, so did my anger. I began to realize that the ongoing crisis' that continued to keep me from being in control in my life triggered the memories of things that kept me 'out of control' in my earlier years of life. I found little relief by understanding the significance between the two events.

The anger that followed these memories severely interfered with relationships of those I loved and who loved me. It hit home that if something wasn't done I could lose self control in all my self anguish.

I finally decided to stop giving into these vices and be more willing to listen to the voice that desperately wanted me to hear these truths, *"You are a woman of great worth and value--Be still and know that I am God"*.

What the enemy intends for destruction - God will use for His good. *God was teaching me how to be still so He could walk me through my past pain and move me forward in His great plan!*

I have learned to cherish this valuable lesson*!*

1. Are there past or present vices in your life that keep you bound in anger? If so, what are they?

2. What are you desperate to hear that would, if just momentarily, relieve you from that anger?

Journey Notes

CHAPTER 3

START THE JOURNEY

The following pages tell a story about Grace having a way of turning an upside down life, inside out.

Growing up as one of seven children presented many challenges in my home. One of those greatest challenges was balancing out equal amounts of love and affection from our parents.

I grew up on a large farm in rural western Kentucky, in a community with only one country store and one church. Many people have described this community as being "the middle of no where." My husband often found a way to slide into his sermons that it was cheaper to marry me than to continue the three day journey to my house and back, while courting me. While the three day journey was a bit exaggerated, we did live nearly 30 minutes from the nearest town on a winding, graveled road that I am certain was only a dirt road not too many years before my arrival into this world in 1962.

Yes, we lived in the "sticks" and we lived up to that title to the fullest. We didn't have indoor plumbing until I was eleven or so. I often laugh about the fact that prior to daddy feeling it was time for us to have the luxury of an indoor toilet; he built a new outdoor "two-seater" to replace the original outhouse which was then falling down. I do need to point out that in the winter months daddy shoveled a path in the snow from our back door to the outhouse for convenience purposes. For my father this was a pretty nice gesture. One can only imagine the reluctance when waking up in the middle of the night and knowing what was ahead would be wading through the sometimes two foot snow drifts during that two-seater, post one-sweater outdoor toilet days. Indoor plumbing was installed in later years which were eventually followed with the warmth of an indoor bathroom.

Money was very limited in our home and shopping was only for necessities. Due to the distance, momma was "allowed" to schedule trips to town usually only once a week to cut down on cost for gas. This gave my six siblings and me more than enough at home time, and with much resistance, forced us to be creative while finding things to do to pass our time over the weekends and when not in school. Having neither luxuries nor pleasures was my father's agenda for my siblings and I unless it was one that fit into his world of keeping complete control over what he considered a necessity. For him and fortunately for me, horses were a necessity on our farm. As leisure activities were rarely accepted, I grew exceptionally fond of his acceptance for allowing me to go on long, leisurely horse back rides. This became one of my greatest passions from an early age and throughout my teen years.

Our mother made great attempts to be involved in our lives as much as time would allow with seven children and a husband who found little time to make family involvement a priority. Priorities for daddy would become priorities for all in our home.

The memories of my father's involvement with my siblings and me are demanding and harsh. Demands of hand picking acres of field corn, helping to clear the farm from what was once covered in woodland to provide pasture for livestock, and helping him cut and stack truck loads of fire wood used to heat our home through the winter months was the typical day of fun which he would create for me and my siblings. There were unspoken rules that we were not to enjoy this time together.

Daddy worked hard and took great pleasure in keeping that as his focus. Looking back I am grateful that it would provide food on the table and a roof over our heads, but at the same time my heart feels heavy when reminded there were little efforts to give us a safe place of comfort and refuge. He made no apologies about work taking precedence over a wasted day of play time for us. Memories of my father as a child were not love, but an empty feeling of fear. Having little opportunities to behave like the children we were, eventually led to resentment and offensive behaviors among my siblings.

It wasn't unusual for me to wake up many winter mornings to discover the water pipes beneath our home had frozen solid. Many of those mornings off I'd go, often with one of my siblings at my side, wading through the snow to draw buckets of water from an old well down the hill from our home to be heated for bathing and washing dishes.

In the summer months this same path was used again for carrying buckets of water to the house when the main well, which supplied water to our home, ran dry. It still amazes me to this day that during these inevitable times of summer droughts and winter freezes each year, this spare well was never connected to our water system as a back up water supply. However, what I find as humorous today shifted towards the other end of the spectrum of emotions during those earlier years of my life, as I should point out that these inconveniences were not a norm for my peers.

While I now treasure these inconveniences as strengthening tools for my future, I certainly dared not reveal these indicators of poverty to my peers during those days. So, I became accustom to the life of a shame bound family. I became very good at isolating myself when I could, and disguising the shame when I could not.

1. What do you see when journeying back through your past?

Journey Notes

CHAPTER 4

THE JOURNEY TO TRUTH

Some of the fondest memories of my family were at meal times. The nine of us gathering around the table at breakfast, lunch and supper while enjoying the pleasantries of momma's hot, made from scratch meals provided a much needed break from the stressful days that more often than not flared with high tempers and resentment. Along with having the most delicious meals in the county, this relaxed time together brought me comfort that made things appear that all was well.

Eventually, my mother somehow managed to talk daddy into allowing us to have extra curricular activities outside the parameters of our corner of the world, as long as it involved little effort from either of them. I don't ever remember feeling abandoned by my parents in their lack of involvement, only grateful for the permission to find an outlet outside of our home. Cheerleading, softball and a variety of school clubs throughout high school gave me a sense of existence, which otherwise was not a familiar feeling to me due to the unrealistic expectations that were forced upon me as I grew older.

Momma was our spiritual leader. She faithfully kept us grounded in church services and events, literally, every time the doors were open. No matter what was taking place: prayer service, Sunday school, Bible School, or revivals, we were there. This allowed us opportunity for encouragement and developing relationships with male mentors in our community, as daddy had a view of church as "useless information" that only interfered with his rigid way of thinking.

For me, growing up with six siblings didn't give much time for quiet moments, so I learned at an early age to cherish any opportunity of solitude I had to myself. As I reached my teens, recognizing the need to create my own safe haven was far from a challenge for me. I welcomed the get away from not only the busyness that came with a large family, but also from the sometimes hostile environment that became more common in our family during those days. As we grew older, unrealistic expectations were heightened and it became more emotionally apparent to me that nurturing and protection were absent in the walls of our home. All the while, momma did what she could to manage to share her heart's overflowing love to help compensate for the loss of balanced nurturing and affection. Yes, her heart was huge and I believe she tried to give her best. Still, her inability to understand that the constant need to excuse and cover-up the absence of our father's willingness to care for our emotional needs and to cultivate a safe environment for his family fostered an arena for a shame bound family (the constant need to mask the truths about the destructiveness taking place in our home). This aided to much confusion about meaningful family relationships which also filtered into a distorted belief system about a meaningful relationship with God and His unconditional, agape love, which I didn't find until years later

How I loved taking horseback journeys and getting lost in the woods on our farm. Through this I found my own source of nurturing. I could spend hours riding aimlessly while searching for a way not to have to end the contentment my heart was consumed with when on these journeys. As a child, I was clueless of the reality that in the vastness of those woods, I was actually searching for something that was absent in my life. It was there that I later found a great peace from the chaos that was safely hidden within the walls of our home - never intended to be revealed beyond those walls.

After years of practice, shame bound families are very creative at keeping secrets, and in order to find my own safe haven away from the chaos in our home, I learned to compete with the traits of being shame bound. I also learned to isolate myself from the realities of those secrets.

A journey through the woods was my great escape. I was able to find solitude while walking along the creeks that ran through a large part of our farm. Climbing the large rocks stretched high above the creeks, and spending hours there embraced by the rays of the sun gave me a safe haven. In this surreal location, I felt safe to unveil my deepest thoughts in absolute solitude. What peace and strength I felt in the stillness of those rare moments.

When reflecting back on these memories, I am reminded that this was my quest to temporarily disconnect from the reality that was causing me much pain. But some forty years later, I am able to sense something much greater taking shape in my life. What I didn't realize then was God's presence there all along. During those times of refuge, He was embracing me with the strength and warmth of His Son as I innocently rested on that solid rock. His presence was keeping me safe from all interferences of the raging waters I desired to leave behind during my escape. Yes, He was there all along whispering to me these passages to recovery, "Be still and know that I am God".

Many like myself, have a story, a testimony of the unexpected moments when God's presence surrounds us while in deep desperation for refuge and strength. Even when we're unaware of our search for Him, He shows up. His presence may not be recognizable until we are able to see evidence of His provisions. These provisions may be as simple as a solid rock to rest on inviting us to be still and embrace the voice that will lead us through passages to our recovery.

There is a Rock that so desire to hold us with the warmth of His Son. This Rock offers peaceful waters flowing from the throne of God, the Lamb, whose words are always trustworthy and true, whose words continue to whisper to those who are patient and listen.

1. Do you ever remember feeling a pressing need for refuge and strength?

2. If so, what were the circumstances you needed to escape?

God is our refuge and strength, an ever present help in times of trouble. Therefore we will not fear though the earth gives way and the mountains be carried into the sea. Though its waters roar and foam and the mountains quake with their surging. Psalm 46:1-4. "Be still and know that I am God" Psalm 46:10

Journey Notes

CHAPTER 5

SPEAK THE TRUTH WITH GRACE

Focusing in on my own personal experiences of what led to chaos, resentment, and hostility described during my childhood and teen years is what guides my story to a life of hope filled substance that will point others to healing. When weighing out the options in how much information I choose to disclose in the pages of this book I discovered much satisfaction in placing more focus on the freedom I received when taking the steps to rid myself of the nearly fifty years of instability described throughout the chapters you just read. I would be remiss if I did not share that in the end it is not the details, but the outcome that holds the substance. To clarify what this means to me is that after repeatedly processing these uncomfortable details, trying to make sense of the what's and why's, I now have the realization that it's more important that I begin to rid myself of what had been polluting my heart while allowing my mind to be consumed with the details that lead to no positive outcome.

A more graceful approach to this belief I have so gladly embraced is one given to me by Care for Pastors Ron Cook, and his precious wife Rodetta. This couple simply encouraged me to vomit up these details that have become my soul's disease, and then reminded me that the solution to being free of any disease requires major surgery. I was instructed by this couple that in order to be set free from the weight of these heavy details in my life, I 'd have to purge any destructive coping patterns that led to my disease and replace them with something else. So, having the understanding of my two options of either being stuck in these details for a lifetime, and at a great cost to my well-being if choosing to do so, or choosing to surgically remove what has caused my disease, I gracefully began vomiting up the heavy weight that had been interfering with everything I strongly desired to be emotionally and relationally linked to: my marriage, my children, my extended family, and even my worship with God. No, regurgitation is not pretty and not easy which may make it easier for some to choose to remain stuck with the weight of the past details. However, for me the effort of doing so brought a great amount of freedom, as the replacement of being rid of this weight led to a positively, beautiful outcome.

Particularly beautiful is that I've been allowed to see into the hurting heart of those I once viewed as the cause for the heaviness in my own heart for so many years. This insight from God has allowed for new growth in my relationship with not only my earthly father but also others whom I'd kept a safe distance from due to the shame that entangled my life throughout the years. I should acknowledge here that this same level of growth may not be the outcome for everyone. For their own reasons, some will choose to continue to remain absent from a severed relationship, while others may have that choice made for them by their offender, be it a relative or other.

Whether the choice is from the recipient, the giver, or both, I want to offer to you that your heavenly Father does not desire for you to remain stuck in the past details of your life. Rather He is there now, as He has been all along, waiting to hand deliver to you the same amount of freedom that He gave to me. This great deliverance came not a moment too late as just months after receiving this great gift of forgiveness, my earthly father began fighting to hold onto what little quality of life that would remain in him until his death in the near months to come. Choosing to undergo the necessary surgery during my journey prior to this sudden turn in his health, has brought me glorious freedom from the heavy weight I once carried by more adequately being able to share with my father what I felt was appropriate for him to hear in his final days.

Many times throughout the previous years these thoughts have played in my mind, "How will I deal with the pain I will have to face when my father takes his last breath?" The loss of a parent is never easy, but for me it seemed as if I would have to face my own death because it would also mean confronting the realities of trauma in my past, which I had fought hard to escape all these years. I now know that had I not taken the steps necessary at the very time I did in finding freedom to forgive my father from the damage brought on by his choices, would have brought me more grief than I could bare when facing these final days with him. These steps brought me to a place of safety when forced to sort through the pain of our past during those final days with him.

The message intended here is a message of what led me to a great understanding that recovery was not only meant to be about me--my greatest discovery during healing and recovery is just that simple--*It was never solely about me!!!!!!*

Therefore, my intention for sharing pieces of my background is neither to place a focus on tearing down those who have brought me pain nor to focus on intimate details within my story. Rather, it's to provide hope to others who are still sorting out issues within their own life's story and who are still resistant to their journey toward healing. My desire is that you will achieve a similar outcome that sets you free from those visuals that tend to keep you stuck on the weighty details that hold no substance, but only aides in spreading the disease.

With this being said, instead of including intimate details of what I endured in my life that brought me to this place of healing, I've chosen to focus on the freedom I am now living out in my life, regardless of what I was forced to endure while getting to the place I am now. In order to effectively do so I have included in the following chapters what have been valuable learning tools that have given much clarity in my own stages of healing from my childhood and other difficult stages throughout my life. Learning tools that would have perhaps been extremely beneficial had they been given to me years before I began searching for understanding of who I really am, who I was created to be, and how to live that out in truth.

I'd often find it difficult to articulate my true feelings or to verbalize them if asked. I've now come to realize that usually this difficulty is due to not having our needs nurtured in the earlier years of life; leaving us to believe our needs have little or no value. In turn, we tend to overlook nurturing our own needs; resulting in neglecting our well-being.

Below are questions to stimulate your thoughts and allow you to process your true feelings. Let these new found feelings and thoughts move you away from any emotional numbness you have developed over the years. Taking valuable time to answer these questions and others in the upcoming chapters can help you to understand your emotions and feel comfortable in sharing them when the time is right.

1. What led you to this open this book?

2. What do you hope to gain from it?

3. What past relationships do you visualize having opportunity to develop a new level of growth?

4. What past relationships have you lost or feel are broken beyond repair?

5. Do you want deliverance from these losses regardless of whether the other party would choose to have deliverance?

6. Are you willing to work for deliverance from this brokenness? Why or why not?

This is a safe place where you can speak the truth with grace. Still, if it is too difficult to let go of the weight of these details at this time turn to the "Journey Notes" at the end of this chapter and make a note to yourself to consider coming back to these questions later after you are better able to process your emotions.

Journey Notes

CHAPTER 6

LEARNING TO "BE STILL"

Years ago God began confiding in me, sometimes through very clear verbal communication, how He would use my past pain as gain in the years to come. I didn't always understand the process, but I was always very certain about His promise. One particular time that stands out above many was while I was simply standing at the kitchen sink washing dishes. With no thoughts on my mind concerning my future, a voice came out of nowhere saying to me, "I am going to use you to speak my truths to help other women and their families".

I stood there for quite a while asking myself, "Did God just speak to me"? I heard it again only this time more clearly, "I am going to use you to speak to my truths to other women and their families". Being unsure of it's meaning, and completely overwhelmed by the realness of this voice, I ran downstairs to my husband and told him the plan I believed God had just spoken to me. My husband was a firm believer at that time, but not convinced that God had communicated with me in the way I perceived it. I suddenly learned the meaning of a personal experience with the Lord and I had to accept that I didn't need the approval of others in order to trust what God wills to do with my life. These years later God continues to affirm to me His promise while needing me to continue to confirm to Him, through my acts of obedience, my complete trust in His guidance.

At that time I had been collaborating with schools in the surrounding communities through 'See You at the Pole' youth rallies and spear headed a community 'Stand Against Violence Effort'. Our children were young and I was a proud stay-at-home mom who was thrilled to be involved in areas that could positively impact future lives of our youth in this small way. I had no clue that God used these times for shaping and preparing our future for greater task. Even after hearing His voice so firmly and clearly, I still couldn't comprehend how later my life would be changed by serving others for His purpose.

God has allowed me to use His truths in the lives in children, teens, parents, and in their relationships in the capacity I had never dreamed of in previous years. I never felt the need to question why I am to mentor and minister to those He see's fit to place around me. When it's about God, it's not bragging and if there is one thing to brag on is that I am in total awe of how He has shaped what was once only a passion of mine into a full time ministry resource for Him to use in ways that will bring healing to others.

You may be wondering why God has allowed you to experience certain things in your personal life that have caused so much discomfort for you or your family. Some will say that we are not to question God. I believe whole heartily that His authority is to be honored and reverenced. I also believe that God wants to hear from us so He can communicate back to us.

> *Jonah 2:12 tells us this, "In my distress I called out to the Lord and he answered me. I called for help and you listened to my cry."*

Perhaps asking him questions such as why he allows us to experience certain things will eventually lead to believing that nothing is beyond His arm's reach. If we're willing to listen to His response and then follow His guidance when waiting patiently to hear His still small voice, then maybe our "why me" questions is not selfish at all.

After years of waiting patiently for His response to my own repeated questions of "why me", not only am I able to share my personal testimony of how God guided me through my pain but also share testimonies of others who have walked through their own pain because of my decision to be obedient to God's purpose for me.

I received a call from a young lady who was court ordered to attend parenting sessions. During her time with me she began having memories of her abusive childhood that at that time had required her to be raised by her aunt and uncle.

Often this woman's mother was in and out of her life. The aunt and uncle was finally convinced by my client's mother she had made a life change and asked their permission to take her daughter to another state to live with her. The young woman described to me how she desperately desired to have her mothers love and managed to convince her aunt and uncle to let her go. She shared with me how her mother began allowing her at this young age to use cocaine with her in exchange for using her body for luring men that would support her mothers drug addiction, and then taught her to steal for what they needed when there no men available to support them.

After her aunt and uncle's awareness of this abuse and neglect they won the battle to bring her back to their home. The loss from once again being abused and rejected by her mother caused this young woman's life to quickly spin out of control. Her following years were spent being consumed by drugs, repeatedly being physically and sexually abused by the men whom she only searched for acceptance and love, and later led to losing parental rights to all four of her children.

Realizing some drastic changes had to take place in order to not lose her rights to the baby she was now carrying, opened doors for me to help her see how she had only been repeating the generational cycle which was handed down from her mother's inability to show her love. What she had been dealt with in her younger years was shaping her own choices during her adult years and destructively robbing her of the ability to love and nurture her children in the way she now desired, and the way they most definitely deserved.

By the end of our sessions there were indicators of what might be a positive outcome for her future. As her children were slowly being transitioned back into her care, one at a time, she was also showing indicators of hope that healing could take place, and would no longer remain stuck in the ruts that kept her from experiencing the glorious freedom to live her life the way God intended her to.

During these circumstances and many others, I consider it a privilege to be a tool that can help shape the lives of those whom God chooses to put in my path. God clearly uses these opportunities to reveal His answers to the many times I have personally asked "Lord, why me", when in my own times of confusion and discomfort. I am so thankful that God wants to hear from us-I am so honored that I am allowed to hear from Him!

Whether standing at the kitchen sink with no expectations of God showing up, or on your knees praying for deliverance from what life throws your way, God will direct your path when He has your attention to listen and then follow His lead. Understanding His purpose for our challenges takes patience and this simple action-- "Be still and know that I am God"!

1. Have there been times God was trying to speak to you and you turned Him away?

2. If so, reflect now on what message you believe He wanted you to hear and how you would respond to that message today if given a second chance?

Journey Notes

CHAPTER 7

ADAPTING TO THE TRUTH IN TIMES OF INSTABILITY: GOOD TIMES / BAD TIMES

Anyone who has unfortunately experienced trauma, has also had opportunity to understand that to grasp onto something to help us to cope with the impact of this trauma, is a vital part of survival. As a coping mechanism, it is easy to choose to be deceived by the less intense or less painful times in our lives, in comparison to other times which brought about a much greater amount of pain. We can then more easily mislabel those less painful times (or memories) as being "good times"-- memories that are easier for our hearts to embrace. Doing so allows us to justify any normalcy in our lives, through our perception of what we view as normal in the lives of others.

An example of the justifications just described is the misguided perception from memories of togetherness in my own family, such as working together on our farm and our parents faithfully making it a priority to have family meals together around the kitchen table, whether free of conflict or not. This mistakenly led me to beliefs of having a life of somewhat normalcy in my family when reflecting on these times together. These beliefs can easily be viewed as "good times" when compared to memories of hostility and broken relationships that were otherwise, and at other times, present in our home.

The visual of our family members connecting while sharing what can be two very strong areas of bonding for many families (chores on the farm and gathering for family meals) may seem deceiving if there was no mention, or no memories, that our family often experienced hostility and sometimes verbal, emotional, and physical abuse, that led to unspoken realities often taking a front row seat over acts of love and affection. I chose to be deceived by refusing to acknowledge the existence, or even the severity, of these unpleasant realities that took place within our home.

Like many, the awareness of damage that developed during my childhood had not become visible to me, until a time of instability in the later years of my life. This time of instability triggered old wounds that for the first time would undergo a series of emotional surgeries due to the length and depth of my denial. However, as a great relief, I now can be thankful in knowing that for years this denial became my defense mechanism protecting me from the overwhelming anxiety that was too great for me to acknowledge and cope with at that time.

We learn to adapt to harsh environments by giving permission to ourselves to be changed by these environments. As long as we can hang on to any seemingly "good times" (memories that bring meaning in our lives), then we justify disguising the anxiety, shame, or guilt brought on by any less desirable parts of our lives we would have chosen to erase, but could not. I adapted to my environment by accepting the seemingly "good times" in our home as a replacement for denying the bad. It was through my defense mechanism that I could better cope with the uncertainties of each day.

In summary, we choose what memories we can handle, and deal with safely, and permit the rest to become invisible—locked away in the unrevealed, secret compartments of our hearts.

Adaptation becomes part of our coping mechanism.

Maybe you've never taken the time to know the harmful solutions you have turned to in order to cope with (or "fix") the *destruction* that has taken place in your own life. Understanding these behaviors becomes clearer once the mind has been able to work through the realities of what's caused destruction in your life. Take the time here to process what your own environment really did look like while in the midst of your personal struggles.

1. Do you remember finding ways to compensate for what you knew was un-normal behaviors in your home? Was this compensation to protect you or rather to protect others?

2. If so, what actions did you use to disguise the truth? Did you isolate yourself, attempt to prove yourself to be different than who you really were, or turn to harmful behaviors in order to remove yourself from the realities of the hurt these truths brought to mind?

3. Who do you hold resentment toward for not speaking truth to you and instead insisting you mask the truth in order to cope?

4. How does it feel to consider speaking these truths now?

Journey Notes

CHAPTER 8

WHO AM I?

Before we travel any further this is a good place to look at the paths you will take as you continue to read. What would you discover if you journeyed through your own personal past? Before you begin this chapter take time out to look at that. Write what immediately comes to your mind in what you expect you will discover about yourself while taking this journey.

Use the space below, or, if you fear that someone may read this book, keep a notebook handy, or you can include these writings in your daily journal as many of these chapters will ask you to express your thoughts. If you've not started a journal this is a great time to do so.

Really! Take the time here to write your immediate thoughts, and not what comes to mind that would make you feel more secure if only you could avoid the truth about yourself. Don't be held back by energy zapping fears that want to take control or replace those very real emotions rushing through your mind. Healing can begin now. It will be interesting to see how you are able to express yourself in ways you had never before had privilege to if going back and re-reading your thoughts once you complete this book. Doors to great discoveries may open about yourself which you never before knew.

Let healing being now!

There are common threads that I believe are among many who have personally experienced destructive patterns. One of them is a damaged relationship with a parent. The negative impact of this loss and rejection not only alters your own emotional needs from being met, but the entire family's relationship can suffer. Trying to maneuver around this missing component can bring on a load of confusion that at some point will trickle into the emotions of family dynamics as an entirety, and eventually aide to dysfunction if not attended to appropriately.

The impact from the absence of a parent/child relationship can take shape in many forms of poor choices throughout our lives--all of which are a means to attempt to replace something missing. Our victimization may lead us to the false belief that our choices are not actually ours to make at all. The remainder of this chapter will lay out the foundation that can guide you to see how you can re-gain full ownership of your choices.

You can choose to avoid pain and suffering by attempts to escape the reality of what really occurred in your life or by grasping onto memories that make you feel normal in order to mask the damages that actually did take place. You may recall the example I gave earlier when sharing memories of my childhood that our family meal times and shared chores on the farm gave me some sense of normalcy (at least from my own perspective) while we shared the togetherness that made us appear to be living as a healthy family to those on the outside. In my adult years I have since discovered that unintentionally I've implemented these same false truths while raising our children. I had developed the idea that the relationships within our home will not survive outside of our home, unless certain tasks were practiced and certain expectations were met that others could witness. A clear but silent message of approval was waiting to be received by those outside the walls of our home of what I'd created my ideal family to be.

Yes, there were strong efforts on my part to create an unrealistic perfectness such as what had been modeled to me--though under different circumstances. Still, the impact can be just as damaging. This was never an intentional choice. All along I thought I was providing a healthy foundation of boundaries and nurturing for my children to build on when faced with making tough choices in their future. I have since discovered what was happening. I was so focused on my own insecurities of what was withheld from me as a child that I neglected to provide the consistent, unconditional love and security they needed and desired.

My three children, now adults, have very honestly and openly let me know about this emotional neglect that took place in our home. I, on the other hand, was not as honest about these truths with myself, in the beginning stages of their need to confront me with the very real anger and control issues they had witnessed from me in their earlier years. It wasn't until I was forced to face the reality of neglect and abuse that took place in my own years of childhood that its impact on my children and husband were revealed to me. What I discovered was I was not the person I thought I was, and definitely not the mother, nor wife, I was called to be. But in time, it began to make perfect sense! I had hit a moment of truth and the pill I had to swallow before I could process the reasons behind this truth was a hard and bitter one.

Growing up in a dysfunctional, abusive home made it difficult for me to filter through not only my needs that were not adequately met as a child, but also the most in-depth needs of our children that arose during the times of their personal experiences of family crises. This lack of filter clouded my ability to overcome a self imposed perfection that I subconsciously thought was needed in order for me to protect myself and my children. As intentional as I was in wanting to provide nurturing for our family, I missed the opportunity to tend to the individual emotional needs that my children really craved while effortlessly sorting out my own emotional needs. Whether from the absence of nurturing in my own childhood or from the battles our family continually faced from their earliest years, the truth is, I was there in person but often absent in mind and heart. I now see that my self-efforts of false nurturing became a chore my children had to earn. My inability to nurture in the way most desired resulted in resentment in my children's adult years.

Perhaps I am introducing another book when I mention these false truths I so carelessly practiced with my children, yet I am trying to understand why the need to share this now. Here is what I have come up with.

Throughout my life while trying to sort out who I was suppose to be to others, I had written my own book of instructions that was only pleasing to me. Eventually I discovered I was the only one who was willing to be a participating character in this book. I was mistakenly repeating that generational cycle of what I have since learned is called "shame bound parenting". In other words, all who looked in from the outside would, without a doubt, know that "all was well in my home", regardless that it was not always well. What should have been a priority of sincere and consistent guidance toward spiritual and personal growth for our children was confused with, and at times replaced with, effortlessly working to prove to myself and to others that I could be a successful parent and wife if I can be perfect, or in truth, *LOOK PERFECT!*

The message in my book of instructions which my children and husband had become very aware of and later grew painfully tired of, stemmed from the shame and guilt which I had been predisposed to from my earlier years. So, at the end of the day I was using my family to create a self-made family of perfection in hopes of masking what I didn't want to confront about myself. I felt loved when I was at my best and not worthy of love when I was not. Was this false belief being passed down for my children to learn? Was this only another chore I had created for them to achieve in order for them to feel my love? I am afraid it was!

Even though I've since worked hard to break that destructive cycle to one that will free me from shame bound to shame free living, the consequences that resulted from my confusing and inconsistent expectations were costly! Much effort was required during the heartache of walking our sons through years of intense recovery from addiction and issues of mistrust; my marriage had begun to show strong evidence of corrosion. These challenges resulted not only from my emotional difficulties but also my husbands own difficulties due to the impact of personal losses he experienced. Eventually my husband was forced to make a very tough decision concerning his position as senior pastor in a church in efforts to protect the church from knowing and becoming infected by the difficulties in our home. The years that followed required a great amount of work in rebuilding sincere relationships for our entire family based on solid truths.

I was forced to hit that dreaded moment of truth and had to be willing to do the work in taking responsibility for my own personal healing and recovery (no matter how hard it would become). When time came to count the cost, the realities in the risk my family would be facing proved to be huge!

Our choices will inevitably leave a mark, whether its target is our children, or others. I had to choose not to get caught in the web of cycles that are often repeated in families through generational brokenness. With much gratefulness, I came to recognize the damage I was causing by holding on to these false beliefs that I once thought were required of me in order to prove my love and to be loved. Still, recognition is only the first step--there is much work to be done.

Though still weeding through some tough spots from the past, our family strives to build our future on solid truths. No longer is there a need to allow past memories to measure my worth and value of what was and was not. In other words, I no longer need to search for nor eliminate a particular memory that will measure the weight of my worth and value. My heart has been set free from those lies.

There is much hope in my family's future as I now choose to place my hope in something Rock Solid

Do you need to continue holding onto certain memories in your life in order to cancel out your most unpleasant memories? We all have a need, deep down, to put meaning to not only our childhood, but also, our pure existence in any stage of life. The strong caution here is to not allow your search for meaning to be the determining factor of your absolute worth and value. Doing this can keep you stuck in a whirlwind of destructive patterns!

I have discovered that God will replace my pain with gain, and all the while reminding me of the perceived "good times" in my past not as denial of the un-pleasantries in our home, but as a true reflection of His love and grace. He reminds me that regardless of what I was handed in my previous years, He was there all along providing me comfort and a positive future filled with enormous worth and value! Remember, grace has a way of turning an upside down life, inside out—moving our hearts toward Him, resulting in deliverance.

Yet there's the question that many will ask--"How we can possibly find gain when we have been treated so unfairly?" The answer I have found is, again, we have a choice. Jesus' gift to us on the cross was not fair, but that sacrifice was a choice He willingly made. We can choose either freedom or to remain captive in chains. To be set free is to be loosed from those chains. When choosing forgiveness toward others who committed wrongdoings against us--taking our focus off of darkness and now setting our sight on the light desperately fighting to find its way in your life—you too will experience freedom.

> ### *"The truth will set you free"*
> ### *John 8: 32.*

Pain turned into gain--

God's word is truth. His word tells us that the mountains may fall into the seas and the earth may give way as many of you reading have witnessed in your own personal life of tragedies. But, in Him we will find strength and refuge that equips us to press forward during these times. Beautiful healing awaits us. We can choose to bring light to our life by holding tight to the only truths that can truly set us free from past hurts. As healing continues, we will see that the greatness of God's love will draw us to an understanding of the greatness in our worth and value. Jesus says, "You are worth dying for."

Pain turned into gain--

Choosing forgiveness may seem an impossible task when relying on our own strength and abilities, which as a reminder, are self efforts that can lead to failures. But when also reminded that God is our strength and refuge no matter the tasks before us, we can trust that He will continue to provide that security when all else feels insecure. Therefore, the choices we make determine the outcome of what the enemy intends as destruction in our lives. I knew I had to learn to forgive those who had brought me pain and suffering. Through this effort I discovered what was meant to destroy can be restored!!!

Pain turned into gain--

Sometimes we just need justification for doing something that seems unnatural......letting go of what we feel such a strong need to protect rarely feel natural. One truth we can believe in is this--Jesus' gift to us on the cross was not fair to the sinless Son of God, nor does it seem natural for our human nature to wrap our minds around, still it was justified. I am so very thankful that Jesus made the choice to let go and let God guide. Letting go of anger and bitterness moves us toward great opportunities to grow, and greater freedom to love.

Pain turned into gain!

During recovery there may come a time when it seems imperative to make it known to those who hurt you that you have chosen to set them free. This does not have to be done verbally. Actions can speak volumes that may later open doors of verbal communication when it can be more appropriate and necessary to verbalize this forgiveness.

The one who offended you may also choose to not accept your invitation to mend a broken past. As difficult as it may be, if this is their choice, decide before hand not to allow this to discourage you from keeping your mindset on the truths of rock solid passages that will point you to an ever growing recovery. During times of challenges our tendencies are to lose hope that our lives' circumstances could never change. We can be assured to know that choosing to remain on this path less traveled--seeking forgiveness--will secure us of no chance of falling into a rut that will keep us stuck in self-contempt toward selves or of others any longer.

Restoration is available and waiting. Before we can experience it in its fullness we first have to give ourselves permission to receive it in faith. Faith will manifest into the freedom we desire and deserve, no longer imprisoned in false beliefs.

Let these passages to recovery be your rock solid foundation to the beginning of your restoration.

> *"The truth will set you free; if the son sets you free, then you are truly free." John 8:32, 36*

These are truths you can begin building on. When you find it easier to give up hope that change could ever take place (there will be days you will), go to these truths. You will need these rock solid passages to recovery in your life to stand on as you continue to push through the pain.

1. From what do you need to be set free?

2. Is there anyone in your life you need to forgive?

3. Is there anything which you need to forgive yourself?

Journey Notes

SECURE YOUR JOURNEY

The best planned journeys are ones that will bring opportunities to explore, make discoveries, and help our minds to grow to a new level of awareness through these discoveries. It's difficult to know how to prepare for a journey unless you have some insight on what to expect ahead of time. Helping you to be prepared for what's ahead is what I hope to help you with as you continue through this book.

In the last chapter we looked at searching for meaning in our good memories, while blocking other memories that were not safe. Chances are, the farther you travel, the deeper the layers of unpleasant discoveries you will uncover.

At first glance, blocking out these areas in our lives makes sense when the need to protect our hearts is so great. Still, you may remember that at some point continuing this practice of coping becomes destructive as the weight of these heavy details becomes our disease. The process of ridding ourselves from this weight is replacing the weight with something else that is easier for us to carry. This is the process of transferring what's been locked deep within your mind and shifting it over to that safer place in your heart where healing and recovery can slowly take shape.

While pressing your way through those difficulties your heart will let you know when the weight is once again too heavy and you need a break. Pay attention to this. These discoveries, as uncomfortable (and at times painful) as they may be, will help us to see where we once were and what can be accomplished if we continue to move forward in our recovery. This is a valuable part of our healing!

Each of us has a personal story that, when we allow ourselves to go there, will define the road toward our journey. For some that journey might start at a time when your life had been unwillingly stretched by the reality that shaped only a false existence from an early age. On the outside you managed to keep a steady, but cautious pace in both your steps and your conversation. You may have been able to disguise anyone from discovering that your earlier years of life had ever been anything but normal. There were times that even you could be convinced of a somewhat self-portrayed fairy tale. While on the inside there was no disguising the truth that much of the time your worth and value was only held by a thread of hope that someday you could possibly live out that fairy tale. But today remains a brokenness that is far too familiar--a life of secrets that you believe would kill your soul if you permit yourself to purge them out: a life of destructive patterns.

What is your personal story?

Some may have managed to hold it all together for a while before the structure of life's foundation began to crack for various reasons. You may have endured a broken marriage which ended in a bitter divorce, experienced the death of someone you loved deeply, or a life threatening illness has consumed yours or a precious loved one's life. You may have fallen victim to an unspeakable crime committed against you, or watched helplessly as your child chose the path of their own destructive lifestyle. Or, perhaps yours is a story of facing strong consequences from poor choices and finding no hope of forgiveness from others, yourself, or even both. These and other life altering circumstances alone can be unbearable. But for victims of trauma any of these heart wrenching circumstances can trigger memories of past trauma leaving an even greater opportunity for the enemy to sabotage our weakened minds and convince us of no hope in continuing to fight for.

Regardless of the situation that led to your journey, if not dealt with can result in your life being lived out in painful silence that can lead to patterns of vast destruction. Whatever the path that brought you to the realization of the need to be set free, the path has not been an easy one. Knowing this, I want to remind you of these passages of hope.

> *God is our strength and refuge, an ever*
> *present help in times of trouble.*
> *Therefore we will not fear though the earth gives*
> *way and the mountains fall into the sea.*
> *Though the waters roar and foam and the mountains*
> *quake with their surging. Psalm 46:1-4*

1. What is your initial response to hearing the words to these passages? Relieved, confused speechless, or other?

2. Being completely honest with yourself, did you hear a personal message through the words in these passages?

3. If so, what message was spoken to you? We tend to be more truthful when we don't give ourselves time to think about what we would say if aware that someone is hearing us or else will later be reading our thoughts. Write it as it really is—-this is for no one but you.

If you did not hear God speaking to you when you read the above scriptures, then please go back and re-read them like this:

> *God--our refuge--is a place of security. He wants to be our refuge and strength--when all else is insecure. He is always there, when everyone or everything else fades, to help when we are in trouble: whispering these sweet words, "Be still, rest in My strength while knowing that I am God. I created you and have great plans for you." At that moment we need nothing more than to acknowledge that there is nothing He can't do.*

Through acts of self-contempt, you might have had thoughts that, "These words may speak truth for others, but could never apply to me". If you believe you are unworthy of these words holding any truth for you, know that it stands true for you, as well. God wants to be "your" refuge, even at times when you've labeled yourself at a lesser value and undeserving of that kind of great and awesome love.

These are passages that will lead you into experiencing the freedom of glorious recovery from your times of trouble.

4. What source of refuge do you think of turning to when you are in need of comfort?

For example:

Is it a healthy resource (i.e., close family member, trusted friend, pastor, sincere prayer, Bible reading, or morally sound books?)

Or can this source lead to destruction (i.e., abusive or unstable family member or friend, contacts that have no personal interest in your well being, feel-good books or magazines that will only bring temporary satisfaction, drugs, alcohol, or other acts of abuse?)

5. Why do you choose this particular resource when in need of refuge?

He is Strong, Mighty, and Faithful.

This description of God was given to me from eight year old Olivia when asked what God meant to her after boldly sharing with me her acknowledgement that God is there to help her deal with her fears. I hope these three words from this wise eight year old, filled with wisdom beyond her years, will minister and reinforce truth to you, as they did me. God is strong enough, mighty enough and always faithful to protect "you" when confused and in pain from the destruction of "your own" experience that is unique to no one but "you." There are no exclusions in this passage; it applies to all, even "you!"

Whether or not you are ready to accept this is up to you. It was no accident that you picked this book up.

6. What circumstances, past or present, have left you experiencing the earth below you crumbling? Mountains around you falling?

7. Name a time when you felt you were drowning in waters so strong with rage it seemed it could have made even the mountains quake?

8. What are you really searching for that led you to have interest in this book? I encourage you to honestly write out these thoughts while they are fresh on your mind.

Journey Notes

CHAPTER 10

HOW DO I HEAL: UPSIDE DOWN OR INSIDE OUT? IT'S NOT AS CRAZY AS IT SOUNDS

As you move through your recovery, wouldn't it be much easier to have a sign, or even better, a little instruction book to give us the best direction to help avoid the experiences that bring about unbearable heartache? I can't count the times I've heard people say, "I wish I had a sign right in front of me that would say turn here so I won't have to wonder if I'm making the right decision". If being honest, most of us have wondered if such a fool proof path exists. Even better would be a sign pointing to the path that leads to a life of complete joy, purpose, and worth.

For some, having any knowledge of joy, purpose, or worth is so far away from reach, that to understand its meaning is not accessible. How then, do we understand what signs to look for when our hearts desire is to follow that path? Where do we start when we so often have to face the obstacles brought about from others whose perception of us is based on what they think we should be or do? If your heart has been wounded (particularly from those with whom you have strong ties) this evaluation can be a huge part of what's keeping you stuck in the heaviness of past experiences? The truth is that many of us do not need others' perceptions of how well we measure up; when we do that destructive job so well ourselves.

1. Joy, purpose, and worth--what does that look like to you?

2. When is the last time you were able to use these three words to describe your life?

Picture a place you would go that would allow you to know the freedom of just being you. All those who kept you from having this freedom (those who are obstacles in your life) are not permitted to go with you.

This is kind of like the freedom women find when not worrying about having to wear makeup for fear of how they will be viewed in their "realness" without it. While this may seem like a poor analogy, we do have complete freedom to be ourselves when no one has the opportunity to place value on us based on outward appearances. Let me explain that when I mention our outward appearances, I am not only speaking of our facial beauty or appearances of our body or even where we live work, or our accomplishments. Outward appearances consist of anything other than what makes up our inner character, and that only comes from the heart. This type of judgment creates obstacles that keep us from expressing the freedom of joy, purpose and great worth we are all created to experience inwardly and desire to express outwardly. The reality for some is the obstacle of how you view yourself, and not allowing you to be just that--yourself, with no need for added fluff to cover up flaws. For many of us having fear of being just who we are is very real and builds a wall to finding the well deserved joy, purpose, and worth within.

3. Who or what in your life has been an obstacle preventing you from having freedom of experiencing who you are created to be? Take time to name those here. If you need more time to process this, the "Journey Notes" at the end of this chapter can be used to remind you to return to this question when you are ready.

The feeling of knowing there is value in your presence takes all the focus off of expectations that rob us of our value.

Terry and I have had opportunity to be guests at pastoral retreats. Being an invited guest in someone's home makes you feel so welcome, that you know your company is not only appreciated, but honored.

Recently we spent a week on a ranch in the mountains of Northern Colorado. This being an unexpected getaway, resulting in having to make last minute arrangements for our ten day stay after driving some 2500 miles from home, we were blessed by the opportunity of a little log cabin being generously provided in such a short notice. Before we ever left home to begin our travels to stay at En Gedi Retreats cabin, we had been informed by its founder Carl Walker that our invitation was clearly based on one understanding. We were told that during our stay we were only to do what was necessary to find relaxation and restoration while there. No strings attached, no "make-up" required, we could be ourselves while doing the job we had set out to do on this journey.

While on our return trip home, my husband and I discussed our desire to have the same heart toward others as Carl did with us-- that is, no strings attached. This trip was one that was needed for intense restoration in our lives after dealing with a heavy season of heartache while reaching out to our son during a time of need for his own restoration.

To break up the long drive home we made plans to stay overnight in Williamsburg, Kansas. Once again, we were overwhelmingly humbled by the generosity from another couple, Randall and Julie Lipscom, who managed the Timberlakes Camp and Retreat Center where we stayed for the night. Like Carl, when this couple knew of our needs, we were given a cabin to lay our heads for the night so we could rest up for the remainder of our trip home. As we got to know this family, it was revealed to us that they had experienced the death of their eighteen year old son just a few years earlier. Yet today the couple still continues to actively reach out to others through their retreat ministry which their son had been so involved in prior to his death--absolute faithfulness and an indication of finding truth in forgiveness.

Having this knowledge gave me renewed insight on how small the difficulties really were that my husband and I were personally dealing with. We had <u>not</u> lost our son. Therefore at that point, anything else seemed so insignificant to me. How much more purposeful our lives are if we become faithful and obedient to the call to serve, when opportunities are given to do so, even in the toughest of trials.

As this journey continues, and not too far down the road from our over night stay in Kansas, we pulled over to a rest stop. While there we spent time talking with a man and his three teenage children who had been traveling from Wyoming after a visit with his dying father. He shared with us the need for gas money to get them back home to Alabama. Initially I wasn't confident we were to reach out to a need that may hold no truth. Just as I was sharing my opinion of this to my husband I was reminded of our conversation only an hour before about our thankfulness toward those who stepped up to help us in our time of need during that week. Suddenly there wasn't much cause for conversation between my husband and me in order to come to the agreement that this was the opportunity to pass on what had been given to us so willingly and graciously from others who knew nothing about our credibility during that very week, but gave anyway. So then, at that moment we decided not to judge theirs.

What had felt upside down in our lives that led us to this long journey only one week earlier was now being turned inside out. All along, this time in our lives was being used to pass on our own great joy, purpose, and worth which had been so greatly strengthened by many both prior to and during that week of travels.

We knew after we prayed, without a doubt, we had been given instructions, "a sign" showing us what direction we were to take in this situation, and not to question the "what if's" we all seemingly want to ask before feeling comfortable stepping up to minister to someone we know very little about. The compassion we received that very week was also a very fresh reminder for us to use our renewed humbleness and to obediently reach out to this family just as we had witnessed others reach out to us in obedience during our own times of brokenness. While we had very little to offer, our awareness had been heightened to the realization that experiencing joy, purpose, and worth was not all about us. God does want us to be good stewards of His gifts, and He has shown us over again that each time we turn to Him for direction when a need is presented to us, even when it does not make sense, then He--God will provide what is necessary to meet it.

During the one and a half hours that my husband and I spent gathered around a picnic table while getting to know this family, it was no longer important to continue with our plans to be home before midnight. Our greatest joy came in the moment of joining hands and praying with this father and his three children over how God would provide for the remainder of their trip home.

You might be asking what this story has to do with your own circumstances that lead to a strong desire for healing. My answer is this: IT'S NOT All ABOUT ME!! IT'S ABOUT WHAT HE WILL DO THROUGH ME. AND, WHEN I ALLOW, THROUGH MY OWN PERSONAL CIRCUMSTANCES I CAN BETTER SEE THROUGH HIS EYES, AND INTO THE HEARTS OF OTHERS!!

My relationship with God was strengthened not only during that time, but many other times, when in similar circumstances. I now know it was only through our obedience that we were able to discover the greatness of joy, purpose, and worth that each of us desires though brought about by an extremely unpleasant and exhausting journey that we would not have chosen had circumstances been different. This story is one of many in which God revealed to me the purpose He has for me while enduring past unpleasant memories. What the enemy meant for destruction, God will use for His good when we allow Him. The truth is, that as each new discovery continues to build our trust in finding worth and even purpose within our lives, sharing this transformation with others becomes less difficult. I find great joy in that, even if I have to discover it through the greatest of storms in my life.

God's Grace has a way of turning everything in life that was once upside down, inside out. The awareness gained for the real purpose of how God ultimately used this trip gave us the desire to find more of what would be in store for us when walking obediently in faith in our home life, our work life, and our interactions with life out in the world. Though this walk will not always embrace us with truth or love, we have a choice to make regardless of what is not given back to us in return.

Visualize how it feels to be someone's guest and immediately upon arrival you are reminded that as a guest the only expectations are that you relax, find rest, and be restored during your visit. Then at your departure you are better equipped to handle what life presents next. A day spa at it's best! Then visualize upon returning back to your own home the strength you gained during this time of restoration allowed you to begin seeing positive changes take shape in many significant ways. We begin to view things in with greater clarity.

If faithfully and obediently we are choosing to follow solid instructions which actually lead to positive results of living a life out loud--then why wouldn't we want to be searching for that book of instructions while in waiting for a miracle "sign" to point us in that direction? What great relief it is to be led to a place of stillness that will take us into complete restoration; a stillness that will transform our lives no matter what heavy circumstances are surrounding us. I didn't offer any details about our situation just described while on our trip and it may seem much less significant than what you are dealing with at this moment. I do want to offer this reminder, that it's not the details that matter, rather the substance we gain when ridding ourselves of what's been polluting our heart.

My hopes are that the meaning of the message--the substance--stands clear. Don't we desire most to know a love that's unconditional, one holding the highest level of compassion that keeps us still in its comfort long enough to finally understand a new perspective of how to more effectively deal with, and then work through, what life has handed us such as the need for a meaningful childhood, we all have a need for purpose in our lives.

4. What discovery would overjoy you to find positive changes as the end results of your long and exhausting journeys?

5. Could it be that a new found joy, purpose, and worth might lead you to witnessing a new beginning of strengthened relationships; even those that once seemed broken beyond repair?

Whether you believe this could be a reality for you or not, what thoughts go through your mind as you think about this?

On the other hand, much weight can be lifted if a certain level of acceptance is discovered that some relationships may never be mended, especially those in which safety is a concern. This may be a discovery that could bring you great peace if you have been personally affected by the guilt that often follows these unresolved relational conflicts in your past.

Healing cannot take its rightful place without complete honesty--and it may take time to come up with an honest answer. Give yourself permission to mark this page in the "Journey Notes" if you are not ready to yet answer the following questions honestly. Return when you feel ready.

6. With whom do you have lost broken relationships?

7. What are the circumstances that led to this brokenness?

8. How has this affected you emotionally? Mentally? Physically? Spiritually?

Journey Notes

CHAPTER 11

OPEN YOUR EYES

Too often, when times of trauma hit, we become so consumed with the heavy details that our ability to focus on areas such as our family, home, or even finances, soon begin suffering. We find ourselves neglecting the treasures we want to guard the most. Trauma related circumstances can take a strong hold on one's life and interfere with what used to be simple daily functioning if not given proper attention along the way to diagnosing the problem area that needs surgery. The power that drives these interferences has to be replaced with something else or we and our family can easily remain stuck in a somewhat dysfunctional state. A divine operation is waiting to be unveiled.

If there is such a thing as a replacement that can safely steer us away from these dysfunctional cycles, then where do we find it? Learning to let go of interferences that alter our path toward healing is not easy until we understand the true meaning of faith, and then know that it can be trusted even when it can't be seen.

Recently our son Bo shared with me a dream he had. In his dream he had realized he couldn't see. Then, he said he felt it was as if God had spoken these words, "Open your eyes".

Could the discovery of a new window in how we view things be that simple? If opening our eyes is all it takes to step out to begin that journey to the freedom that will remove the interference of the dark clouds in which contentment wants to keep us under, then maybe trusting in faith is not as hard as it once appeared.

The more I work among others who are in need of counsel because of trauma related events in their lives, the more understanding I gain of the truth that each person's unfortunate circumstances have similar traumatic affects in the emotional intensity that can be brought upon them. One parent's suffering over a child who has chosen the path of a destructive lifestyle can be as much emotionally crippling "to them' as a parent who has experienced the death of a child. Individuals living years with a spouse who frequently assaults him/her physically, emotionally or mentally can be just as crippled by the impact of emotional instability "in their eyes" as would a child who was exposed to frequent horrific acts of violence that one should never know existed. With the greatest amount of respect and deepest compassion to the parent who has experienced the death of a child, or, to the individual who has been forced to suffer through years of violence, I need to validate before going any further, how extremely difficult it must be to hear anyone voice they know how it feels having to face these heartbreaking experiences unless they have unfortunately experienced these or others areas of trauma personally themselves. Our perception is sometimes seen with plank filled eyes until we too have had to face similar life experiences.

When aware of one's suffering, brought on by a traumatic event (whatever that may be for them individually) I have learned to not question the severity of pain they may feel in their suffering. Their pain is very real and very legitimate, regardless of the comparison to another's circumstances during their own time of suffering.

If we take the time to look closely enough, we can find ourselves more fortunate than the person next door. The weight of our struggles can suddenly appear to be much lighter when witnessing those who's yearning to repair their brokenness is more complicated than what we could possibly imagine. It's true that most of us can easily look around and find others with worse circumstances which can also reveal to us the many blessings that we often overlook. But if not careful, this can be interference to altar a path that's needed for continuing to work toward our own necessary healing.

When our hearts have been deeply wounded we can easily take the role of a sponge for others who are suffering. We tend to run quickly in attempts to help absorb the pain for those who are hurting, while not realizing that this behavior can be an unintentional motive to avoid dealing with issues that brought on our own pain. Even the person with deeply sincere and compassionate driven efforts can fall victim of this, "My past needs were not met, so I'll make up that loss in my life by being there to help meet others needs, and then I can feel loved." This is often what we are saying to avoid the Divine operation that can rid us of our own pain from losses. If measuring the load of another's burdens prompts us to overlook our own need for healing, we will gain nothing.

One of the tools God gave to me while in my recovery was a ministry that would allow me to reach out to teens, parents, and marriages who are struggling with circumstances similar to what I have battled. While always open to opportunities to mentor those in my church and community I wasn't actively searching for this particular ministry. It literally landed in my lap! I am still in awe today in seeing God's great plan take shape in how he knew would eventually develop into full time ministry for HIS purpose!

I never suggest moving away from reaching out to others experiencing a life crisis; God will want to use you to help others in their time of healing. I do want to urge you to "open your eyes." Don't allow emotional hyper-sensitive feelings toward sufferings of others bring you to a place of contentment that could become a substitute for confronting your own demons and preventing you from moving forward. What a gift--to see into the hurting hearts of others. If you have that gift, be mindful to use it carefully and prayerfully while God patiently works to bring you to a place where you can adequately be His hands and feet during others desperate time of need.

Being aware that at times we unknowingly project our pain into the lives of others, in hopes not to have to attend to our own pain, can be a reminder for us to evaluate what our intentions are when presented with this opportunity. Check yourself! Are you practicing a mode of defensive functioning in attempts to reduce your own anxieties of painful experiences--or are you cognitively and adequately ready to be used for another's need of emotional surgery?

I have full confidence in believing we have each been called to reach out to others in their time of need. The right time will come when you are able to be that lampstand for others who are unable to hold themselves up. But, what I have seen and experienced personally is the need to take appropriate steps first to make sure our own personal treasures are tended to before consuming our time with helping others who are experiencing trauma.

I want to caution you in the same way the airline stewardess instructs us just before the plane takes off. If you find yourself crashing, put the oxygen mask on yourself first before attempting to help those who are weaker, or you may not have enough fuel to help them with their survival--thus your treasures will suffer. If not taking time out to care for our own very real emotional needs, then our families, homes, and finances will suffer.

The following chapters will offer more examples of common struggles for those who have experienced trauma and have not yet opened there eyes to a safe place to begin working through it. These areas of struggles named may not target you individually in your own personal brokenness. Still, please allow this time to open your heart to the hope God wants to bring in whatever area personally affects you. Know that you, too, deserve to encounter *complete* healing and recovery. My hopes are that while reading through these pages clarity will be received for all to know that there is no struggle that our Lord has not met, and certainly not one that He cannot change.

God can take hold of each piece in our lives that has been turned upside down and move us to the next level by turning us inside out. Therefore, our focus is no longer lingering on these destructive patterns within us. God will remove what's been polluting us on the inside--to now focus on His Grace--moving it outward, toward healing through Him. God's Grace has a way of turning everything in life that's upside down, inside out.

Experiencing restoration will open the eyes of our hearts to a heightened awareness of opportunities to not only break past our own deep scars, but also to eventually equip us to walk beside others during their season of hardship. Be patient!

1. From what do you need healing? Before reading any further, write out those thoughts in detail here. This will help you as you move through the next steps of your journey.

   Don't rush those thought processes, be still long enough to allow God to pull them out naturally.

2. Do you purposely avoid opening your eyes to find healing and recovery from your past pain? If so, why?

3. What would you see if your eyes were opened?

4. Where is that place you could visualize going that will provide you with a rock so solid that it could carry all the weight of your burdens, if you were willing to lay them out?

Journey Notes

CHAPTER 12

THE TRUST FACTOR

Perhaps there have been great challenges within your closest relationships--a once trusted friend, family member, spouse, or even a child who has distanced themselves from the bond you once had. I want to start this chapter with questions that will hopefully assist you in having a better insight to how well you handle these challenges and where you are capable of taking yourself even in the midst of them.

1. Where did you find refuge when the raging waters began to roar and surge in your life?

2. What, if any, circumstances in your life have placed barriers around you and kept you from having a safe place to turn when in need of refuge?

3. What uncertainties have there been or are you currently facing within your job, home, finances, or perhaps your health?

4. What source can you, without a doubt, rely on to get you through any tough times of uncertainties, when those whom you consider your closest relationships are seemingly disconnected?

You may have discovered when in desperate need for someone to rely on for solid spiritual guidance that even the strongest, most dedicated, and most spiritual leaders, with the greatest of intentions, can face exhaustion and temporarily be unavailable. Some would probably ask, "How can I not trust my spouse, child, or especially a pastor to give me refuge when I am in trouble"? It's not always that you can't trust these loved ones to comfort you. More so, it could be that when these loved ones begin to get worn down with their own "stuff" it leaves them with little energy to hold both you and themselves above those raging waters. We tend to forget that these same storms, if not capped, can also cause instability that leads to destruction in the lives of those we often turn to for help. Even those who hold the greatest amount of love and concern for you can disappoint you, and many times will.

5. So, where does this leave you: discouraged, feelings of loneliness, disappointed, and often feeling hopeless?

6. What is it that you are feeling right now? I am inviting you to name those feelings here.

Regardless of what led you to feel disconnected from these relationships, you need to know that these emotions just described do not have to be your end results.

If you have convinced yourself that your baggage is too heavy to ever find that place of peaceful refuge, then the source you have relied on will soon be sinking with you when those times of raging waters begin to rise. There is a Solid Rock that invites you to relax in His strength, warmth, and even more so, accepts you on unconditional terms regardless of the weight of your load. This Rock will not only rise above any raging waters that may come your way, but will even prepare you for them before they ever hit.

It is so important to know that what you are turning to for direction and strength when times get tough, won't break when the storms begin moving in. Bro. Ronnie Sivell's, a pastor and family friend, has often made claims that if you're not in the middle of a life storm then get ready; you are either heading into one, or just coming out of one. When we think about this statement it's pretty simple to comprehend that these raging waters are unavoidable. Now, believing in this truth make it easier to understand that we can struggle with the heavy load of baggage in life, and still know a life of worth and value, when having the right tools to work with. You've heard this phrase before and it's worthy of hearing again, your past experiences do not have to define your worth and value.

Are you effortlessly looking for that little book of instructions which offer that fool proof path to a life of joy, purpose, and worth as described in chapter 8? It may even be that you find your self in a spin from desperately trying to write your own book of instructions. I'll reiterate again, the problem I have found with this concept is that others involved in my life are only convinced for a short while to be a participating character in my book. It's not long before it's discovered that there is no value in the rules found in TaJuana's book of instructions, which I have put in place for myself and subconsciously insisted others adhere to. There was nothing solid for others to relate to because these self-made rules (or self-efforts) were all about providing for me, regardless of the needs of anyone else.

Self-made efforts will never survive the raging waters that follow when each new storm begins stirring. Keeping in mind the simple truth that these storms are unavoidable, and being mindful that others are going to disappoint us, may be what drives us to put our faith and efforts in instructions that are solid enough to hold us up when each new storm is encountered.

We are frail in our human nature, but made strong through our spiritual creator. Therefore, as much as we want it, there is truth that we really don't have to rely on others to stand with us when catastrophes hit.

7. Read that last sentence again. Can you find trust in this? Why or why not?

8. Who or what have you relied on in the past to stand with you during a catastrophic time in your life?

9. How, then, did you handle circumstances the next time struggles began to rise if this resource were not available again?

10. Did you find yourself wandering with aimless direction grabbing at whatever tool you could reach to help you fix things?

If you answered "yes" to this last question it does not indicate that you are less adequate, rather that you fall into the same category as many of us--we are each created frail in our human nature. We did not create ourselves and will never have the ability to breathe air into the clay of the ground we walk on and watch it come into a living being. Our spiritual creator, however, did breathe life into each of us and will do much more with the life He has given us when we obediently and completely rely on Him. We can become faithful to relying on His instructions--regardless of whether there are others available to encourage us along the way!

Please don't misunderstand; I know so well, and appreciate so much the blessings of having family, friends and spiritual leaders who stand with me when catastrophes take place. It's when I have tried to depend on them for complete deliverance from these catastrophes that I have been forced to understand the reasons behind my failures in finding the true peace I long for. There is only so much our human nature will allow us to do on our own.

What I find strengthening is the discovery of a positive outcome after wandering with aimless direction in search for understanding of my struggles. The time spent aimlessly wandering ultimately led me to knowing the purpose for the struggles which had been handed to me. This truth will be looked at more closely in the later chapters.

This may be a time you'd want to go back and review the answer to this last question. Use this time to write out what wandering with aimless direction meant for you.

11. How did it affect you emotionally, physically, mentally and spiritually?

Use this space to name how you were affected in each of these four areas.

Many of us spend endless hours in search for someone or something to help avoid dealing with the confusion that accompanies when our hearts are left damaged by failed efforts from either ourselves or others. Soon we begin to surround ourselves with the idea that substitution will bring satisfaction. Failed efforts will always accompany if relying solely on our own efforts, or worldly endeavors, to fix things when in search for peace or rest in our hearts, only to find no true peace or rest in any self-focused attempts to change.

During a get away in search of rest from the busyness in my own life, I was listening to the radio and heard an unknown pastor say, "If relying on yourself to find peace you will only find stress; if relying on worldly things for comfort you will only find distress; but--*here's the truth we are really searching for*--when relying on the 'Prince of Peace' for comfort you will truly find rest. Realizing there was a strong message in this for me, I immediately wrote these three points down. As they began resonating in my mind, I soon began to sort out what this meant for me. Here is what I determined.

Self-efforts can include things such as using relationships for self-gain, overindulging in a focus on your outward appearances, a desire for prestige, and relying on money to meet our needs. Worldly things may include drug and alcohol use (a great risk of leading to abuse) glamorous homes, cars or clothes, pornography, even un-meaningful sex outside of the boundaries created for the sanctity of marriage. Both of these categories include things that are to be purchased at a price--you give up something to gain them. If we stop and count the cost we see a sacrifice much greater than the gain.

However, The Prince of Peace, Christ, has already paid the highest cost possible through the blood He shed on the cross; a sacrifice that no human could ever achieve. His great gift freely offers unconditional love and unceasing acts of mercy, while never wearing out nor never fading in strength. All the while His grace covers our failures. So, is there any need to live under the pretense of our self efforts or worldly decisions that will eventually fade? There is no make-up required when living our lives in truth. We are no longer under the disguise of the fluff that we sometimes feel the need to surround ourselves with when falsely bearing witness to others through our worthless accomplishments.

I guess the question we need to ask ourselves is this, "Am I using these areas of self efforts or worldly things, mentioned above, to disguise the flaws within me? Am I disguising those flaws by substituting them with stuff around me in hopes of convincing myself and others that those flaws don't exist? Or maybe I am surrounding myself with this stuff in hopes of escaping the truth of the destructiveness brought on by someone else whom I cannot seem to escape on my own"? Unless you choose to no longer live in disobedience, find acceptance in who you are, and stop trying to convince others of who you are not, the patterns of destruction will continue in your life.

If your answer is yes to the above questions then I praise you for your ability to *honestly* assess what is the hardest thing for most of us to accept-- the truth about ourselves. No matter how hard we strive for perfection, no matter what we turn to in hopes of covering up what we don't want to believe about ourselves, we will never find rest until we become honest with ourselves and obediently deal with the truth.

I love these words of truth, "Disobedience will take you farther than you want to go, keep you longer than you want to stay, and cost you more than you ever want to pay."

There is never any cost nor consequence to pay when our decisions are based on His (God's) guidance alone. When we truly get this, we can then better understand that any substitution is the cheap stuff--the off brand that keeps us from access to having the weight of our failures and poor choices transferred to a safer compartment, than what our own minds can sort out. The Prince of Peace, Jesus Christ, enables us to purge this weight from our minds to that safe place—our hearts--a compartment our loving Savior will not keep under lock and key if turning toward Him for deliverance.

This transformation begins to cleanse away what has been polluting our hearts when allowing our minds to be consumed with the details that lead to no positive outcome. Thus, freeing us to press forward, resulting in a positive change--a heart change.

To go a step further, when we understand that it is a heart change, through obedience in faith, then healing can begin. It's then we can begin to see that healing has the power to remove any chains that keep our minds bound in discouragement, worthlessness, disappointments, and the belief of feeling hopeless in that whatever things we are struggling with can ever change. There is a purpose for any time you have spent aimlessly wandering in your search for freedom.

We are justified by faith—we have peace with God through our Lord Jesus Christ who is our refuge and strength—an ever present help in times of trouble. Through obedience to Him you will find purpose. Obedience leads to faith and peace. The following chapters reveal how these three actions; obedience, faith and peace, compliment one another.

Journey Notes

CHAPTER 13

TRUSTING THINGS NOT SEEN

In order to maintain true and lasting peace in our lives we have to believe in the source that can provide this. This is the part where faith comes in. In some aspects to believe can mean such a small thing. In others, it can be huge. It might be easy for most folks to believe that if we work, bring home a pay check, and pay our bills, then the electric company won't turn our electricity out. It might also be easy for most of us to believe that the sun rises in the east and sets in the west everyday. But for many of us, what cannot be seen can be a difficult concept to grasp. We can clearly see that the lights stay on when our electric bill is paid, and we can equally see that when we look toward the east in the early morning the sun is lying low in the eastern horizon. Likewise, when we face the west late in the afternoon, the sun now lies low in the western horizon. This belief, most will agree. We have faith this will take place each and every day. This is pretty simple to believe, right?

But then our human nature comes into play here again and sometimes it won't allow us to hope for things that cannot be seen or felt. That's when we begin to rely on those sources that are tangible, gained from our self efforts that can leave us disappointed with no permanent or positive outcome. These things we gain through our own efforts will soon lose their strength. We are frail in our human nature.

To believe in things not seen, takes a lot of faith. Or does it? Scripture—God's word--tells us that all it takes is the faith of a mustard seed. From my experience helping with my husband's family greenhouse and garden business, I can attest that there are not many seeds much smaller than a mustard seed. Our lives can draw strength when we see examples of others who have lived through extremely tough situations in their lives and yet survived: physically, emotionally, mentally, and particularly strengthening is when we witness those, who after facing a life catastrophe, choose to remain obedient and continue to grow spiritually.

A client came to me struggling with memories of childhood verbal, physical, and sexual abuse. This woman shared with me the traumatic details of what she endured during years of sexual abuse from multiple family members, as well as trauma from her mothers physically and verbally abusive behaviors. She explained to me that in order to cope with this trauma her own abuse of cutting and alcohol developed during her early teens. This woman described how her drinking would start as soon as she got of the school bus each Friday and ended on Sunday night in time to sober up before resuming the next school week on Monday morning.

After several visits with me she revealed her thoughts and plans for suicide. It wasn't until the age of thirty five she began to realize that the extent of abuse she suffered from robbed her of having hope for anything beyond her immediate reach that could truly replace her pain. At this point she had lost all hope of ever having freedom in finding a source for healing and recovery that would not lose its strength. She was ready to give up.

Desperate and completely broken during one of our sessions she finally accepted that Jesus Christ was the only source that could fill the emptiness in her life by replacing her pain with the great love, mercy, and grace He has for her. She would finally know the unconditional love of a Father, and for the first time in her life she found it in herself to trust others who wanted to surround her with unconditional loving and meaningful support. Within a week after accepting Christ she began attending Celebrate Recovery, visiting two times a week, and agreed to begin weekly sessions with a mental health professional.

While I can't emphasize enough how difficult it was for this precious child of God to take the steps to reach out for help as mentioned above, I can attest to this--she had to admit she was frail in her human nature and acknowledge that the efforts she had relied on for so many years while trying to "fix things" had only left her disappointed with no permanent or positive outcome. I have now witnessed her gradually find freedom to give up her alcohol, her need to mutilate her body, and her thoughts of suicide.

She expresses that she still feels the pain of the heavy weight from her past, but is discovering great freedom in her choice to end the destructive vices that once held her in bondage of the false truths for comfort when consumed by those traumatic memories. She also shares with me her discovery of hope for the future for her eight year old daughter who has been an innocent victim to her destructive choices. Recently I received a message she left from a phone call saying these words filled with pure joy, "I got it! I got my thirty day chip"! She had achieved thirty straight days of refraining from cutting herself. Where she had once found comfort in mutilating her body to relief herself the pain of her past trauma, she is now experiencing glorious freedom to walk in grace!

I see great hope that this friend will allow her past to be used for the good and glory of God as I am honored to witness how grace has a way to turn a messy upside down life inside out! When we choose to follow similar steps of those survivors who we witness persevere, even in the depths of their personal raging storms, evidence of hope becomes more a reality for us. The hope here is that we too can achieve those same positive end results in our own lives. It is so important to surround ourselves with others who can personally model for us how they persevered through extremely tough times and find restoration in their own faith. God never intends for our pain to be wasted and kept to ourselves.

God's word—His instruction book, speaks to strengthen us in many ways and through many circumstances. However, reading God's word may reveal to us a truth we aren't willing to accept. This solid truth is usually not what we are searching for if looking for something to keep us bound in a life of comfort in areas that are otherwise false truths. But a strong reminder is that these false truths lead to destruction. An even stronger reminder: Grace turns everything that gets turned upside down, inside out, and away from our messy ways of trying to fix things and into God's care. Grace can turn anything the enemy meant for destruction to be used for the good and glory of God. Through this process we can indefinitely be rid of our destructive patterns and released of all pain from our past raging storms.

Have you ever stopped to consider what it really means to be released and set free?

1. Take this moment to write about a time when you remember being released from emotional pain.

2. Did you experience a permanent and positive outcome during that time?

3. If not, what would have to take place in order for you to get to a safe place that will empower you to discover freedom from bondage of that pain?

4. How often since have you wondered if you could find relief from the burdens you are carrying today?

What did you do with this thought? Did you stuff it back down into your out-of-sight, out-of- mind compartment refusing to believe it could ever take place? Or, did you begin visualizing ways in which relief could once again become a reality?

5. If you could choose to have one painful memory surgically removed what would it be?

If this question is causing you to want to shut down, then remember these truths from the previous chapter: *It's through obedience in faith that brings healing. It's then that we can begin to see that healing has the power to remove any chains that keep our minds bound in discouragement, worthlessness, disappointments, and the belief of feeling hopeless in that whatever things we are struggling with can ever change. We are justified by faith. We have peace with God through our Lord Jesus Christ who is our refuge and strength-—an ever present help in times of trouble, if and when we are obedient to recognize Him as our deliverer.*

If you can't answer this question in complete truth now, mark this page in the "Journey Notes" and come back to this when you are better able to look at this area of your past.

I cried out to the Lord and He answered by setting me free – Psalm 118:4

Journey Notes

CHAPTER 14

THE BEST PATH IS THE ONE LESS TRAVELED: STAY THE COURSE--YOU ARE WORTH THE JOURNEY!

As we continue to journey, I want to emphasize here how valuable it is to find a safe place to work through whatever struggles life has handed you. That safe place will need to include surrounding yourself with safe people in your family, community, and in a church that will embrace you with meaningful love and support. You will need to seek out those you can trust to hold you accountable while continuing to press forward during your walk in finding the freedom to make solid choices that will steer you away from poor decisions when a crisis sneaks in. When the pain from past experiences surfaces, it can be easy to try and compensate for this pain by resorting to decisions that will ultimately cause more difficulties later. I have found throughout the years of my own personal struggles, and as well as when working with others in need of counsel, that irrational thinking usually accompanies a true crisis situation. It's in our weakest moments that we are more vulnerable in making irrational decisions, or giving in to what others want for us. These choices usually only bring about more destruction in our lives.

The fierce cycle of destruction I am describing throughout this book is one that fights effortlessly to steer us off course. If we have no safety net of support from others to keep us encouraged to stay on a smooth and safe path before the cycle begins to take over, the destruction is even greater.

A closer view of this cycle may look like this. First, we acknowledge our struggles. After we realize that change needs to take place, we come to a place of commitment to seek out help for working through these struggles. Then, when least expected, a crisis takes place once again and spins us right back into our old ways of coping. This "cycle of past pain" has the ability to take control over and over again by speaking these lies, "You are **not** worth the fight. Change will **never** take place. You may as well **give up** trying." Once we ever give in to those lies we quickly find ourselves spinning out of control again.

In chapter one I shared that much of the time our destructive patterns can be so subtle that no one else may ever know they exists, and they can even go un-noticed by the very person who is unfortunate to possess them. But when we do come to a place of recognition that these patterns are what keep us in the ruts of mud and mire, and finally muster up the energy to take the steps that lead us to understand there is a much smoother path to travel if we are willing to fight for it, we must also keep reminding ourselves that we are never going to be perfect in these steps--there will be slips and falls. It is so easy to let these thoughts of slips and falls speak false lies about our being worthy to continue to walk on that smooth path. These lies may be spoken through someone who constantly reminds you of past choices, or maybe a job loss which so falsely sent the message that you'll never be good enough. Whatever it is that you can personally use to fill in your own blanks here, are only false truths sabotaging your belief system about your self worth, with thoughts that "my life will never be any different so why keep trying"? What could be subtle attacks to one person are extremely vicious to someone who has been over powered by another in any form or fashion.

I want to remind you again that we must be cautious with our approach in finding the right key that can effectively unlock the memories that consumed our lives, or risk stirring up a vicious storm we aren't prepared to tackle while trying to escape those memories. In this chapter we are going to take a look at how easy it is to fall into destructive patterns when we avoid choosing a smooth and solid path-- the path less traveled--the path that can more effectively help us to deal with the negative influences that stir up the storms of our past.

Taking that journey through our past is instrumental in helping us create a safer place for healing to begin while removing layers, one at a time, from years of pent-up pain. As the process of healing begins, this journey also prompts us to think more about what we want, or don't want, for the outcome of our future. You are worth the fight it takes to stay the course when life around you begins to crumble. There is a path I want to introduce to you that is smooth and accessible when understanding that you too can attain better choices for the outcome truly desired.

Choices we make can be a huge factor in determining how much worth and value we place on the outcome of our future. Before reading any further, take some time to think about what it is you really do want for yourself in 1 year, 5 years, or 10 years from today. This time will pass as long as we remain on this earth. That's a reality we can't escape.

Before answering these next questions please allow yourself ample time to think about how you can answer in complete truthfulness. I invite you to remove the masks you have unknowingly carried in attempts to avoid confronting your hurt, and thus allowing your belief system of self to become an easy target for sabotage.

1. What will you expect your life be like at that point?

1 year:

5 years:

10 years:

2. How will you plan to get there?

3. What obstacles have kept you stuck and hinders you from meeting that goal?

4. What will it take to move past that obstacle?

What source are you turning to when in need of support and comfort when challenges take place? Are you looking for comfort in sources that will move you toward a solid future, those that are tried and true? Or do you find yourself settling for what ever falls your way, a quick fix solution?

We have an unlimited amount of exposure to self help information advising us in nearly any situation we may find ourselves. I can find loads of media resources at fingertips reach ranging anywhere from gardening to woodworking (both areas I enjoy doing in my spare time). My point is that for the most part media resources can be extremely useful. But, if not careful, what we choose to turn to for help with decisions in our lives can also be an enemy to our recovery.

Social media, for instance, can not bring us adequate long-term comfort as a replacement for healing. It's true that use of online sources can be a great way to stay in contact with family and friends, but, through the convenience and temptations of questionable web-sites or when giving a particular person of the opposite sex privileges to your secrets of your heart, that no one else has any awareness of, can also draw us into a trap of addictive desires or emotional love affairs when we are most vulnerable.

If our search for help has no solid foundation for building a solid future, then we will likely face un-invited consequences from the outcome gained. Self help is all around us. In truth, some self-help materials are only helpful if your goal is to be self-centered—-after all the term is "self-help". Perhaps this is a more tactful way of saying this--if placing your faith in a source that promote self satisfaction through instant gratification, you will only continue that old cycle of coping (a precursor to patterns of destruction.)

Acceptance of new and effective coping mechanisms is a crucial step in finding a solid future of healing and recovery. When highly emotional events take place, our mental state does not allow us to utilize safe coping mechanisms. We then tend to act in unpredictable ways, or as mentioned previously in this chapter, our thinking becomes irrational. For the person who has experienced trauma, and never appropriately worked through the impact of the trauma, happiness within is a constant search. Without the ability to accept your own need for healing, and with no solid counsel, pent-up anger will continue to feed as instability continues.

Many fall into the trap of blaming others for their difficulties, while avoiding what we are not willing to accept, or perhaps even understand. Discovering our abilities to take charge and make safe choices can eventually repair our brokenness. If there is no self-awareness of bitterness or anger locked deep within, when attempting to escape the pain in need of healing, then to this person any conflict that surrounds them is often going to be someone else's problem. When this happens we are only giving control to another and keeping ourselves stuck in our problems.

What happened to us is not our fault; we did not choose to be victimized. But choosing to rid ourselves of this victimization has to be our responsibility or else we'll carry a great liability.

Avoiding ownership of this particular area gains us nothing. Yes, I know the great challenge of taking responsibility for what we did not choose in the first place. But my hopes are that you too will begin to see that the liabilities that follow when not taking action are not worth it if choosing to stay stuck in unwarranted victimization. Below are some of those liabilities. Previous chapters have pointed out that those who have been wounded often have difficulty with finding stability in relationships. For some, jumping from one broken relationship to another in attempts to replace the pain from our past with a false sense of being is common ground.

If not careful the resources we turn to may lead to poor choices that can take years to sort out, once made. There is a false belief system by many, which some counselors will even support, that ending our marriages will finally be the answer to our pursuit of happiness without first trying strategies that could save the marriage. Part of this false belief is that we are convinced our problems will end when divorce begins. This form of self-made happiness can lead not only to great destruction to yourself, but also aides to that generational cycle of destruction when children (whether young or adults) are involved. Its impact will affect those you love in ways you may never imagine. If you fall into this category stay the course --you are worth the journey!

It is worth all the time and effort necessary to look deeply into the root of what's driving a wedge between the relationship with you and your spouse. In truth, marriages that end in divorce are not always about the difficulties in the marriage itself. it can also be the result of the individuals searching for happiness within when their needs are never appropriately assessed and steps never taken to help resolve the baggage from their past.

These worldly practices, in which we place our faith for instant gratification, hold no substance. In other words, the above scenarios may sound attractive at some point, or perhaps as the only way out. But, they will never produce the positive results that we wholeheartedly desire in our healing and recovery, as it runs contrary to God's word. If you have already been through the steps of ending a marriage, let me encourage you to know that while my views do not condone divorce, there will never be any intentions for condemnation. Perhaps you had little control over that decision at that time, or the truth could be that you were caught in the same trap so many others find themselves in-- advice was given that there was little hope that your happiness would ever be restored. Despite the reasons you and your spouse separated, you are worthy of healing from the impact it left on your future.

The caution here again is that if we are not careful, the sources we choose to turn to for satisfaction will lead us to failure in our false hopes; a false idea of happiness that will only enable us to continue that destructive cycle. There is nothing solid for our future in advice that only gives us false hopes that result in future failure. You will find no peace until healing takes place. Stay the course--You are worth the journey to healing!

In order to maintain true and lasting peace in our lives we have to believe (have faith) in the source that will produce lasting evidence of peace in our lives. Instant gratification (which is only a shortcut) is not a trustworthy source in finding a peace that guides us toward the path of full restoration from past hurts and failures. This kind of peace can only be attained from obedience in choosing the path less traveled.

Though this path is not the shortest, it is ultimately free of the ruts we often find ourselves stuck in when on the un-level, beaten path of mud and mire we have to travel through when on our self-help journeys. Not only are we free from worry of falling into that repeated rut that lead us to being stuck in those false beliefs from instant gratification, but this path allows us time to fully experience our worth and value which we are often robbed of when not taking the time necessary to sort out what has been keeping us stuck in the details of our life's past experiences. Regardless of how unpleasant our past, this smooth path will more easily direct us through fresh encounters of strengthened faith (and not failure) in our future.

I believe this quote is worth repeating: *disobedience will take you farther than you want to go, keep you longer than you want to stay, and cost you more than you ever want to pay. You have a choice!* I am hopeful that as you move through your journey, you will continue to move forward in truth.

Journey Notes

CHAPTER 15

REAL FAITH–NOT FALSE HOPES

In Hebrews 11:1 scripture tells us that "*faith is the substance of things hoped for and evidence of things not seen.*" When we place our faith in false hopes, it's true that we may experience instant gratification. Still, the reality is that worldly things will fade, the earth will give way, and the mountains will fall into the sea: death and illnesses of loved ones will take place, our jobs may not always be there for us when least expected, we may find ourselves dealing with instability in our marriages and relationships with others. When these times surface, we can better grasp that instant gratification may feel good for only a short season.

Life continues to happen at the most inconvenient times. For those who continue to avoid working through healing from the impact of trauma will, at some point, find that things around you will begin to crumble, raging waters once again begin to consume your mind, and a repeated cycle of chaos and confusion will creep in while attempting to fill the gap with "feel good fluff" that hold no substance. Looking for a new mate for instance, when the relationship in your marriage seems to be fading, may only bring you a new mate to share in new chaos and confusion.

This chapter will focus on similar examples to describe how when faith is absent, we resort to shortcuts to gain instant gratification (some severely destructive) as an attempt to escape what we don't know how to fix. The unhealthy decision making traits listed in this chapter are typical for those who have suffered from trauma and abuse, and have not yet walked through the healing process.

There are times when we become so focused on what areas someone else needs to improve on that the tendency is to overlook asking God to help us to change the areas in which we, ourselves, need improvement. Not only will we fail in the attempts to transform the "other-person" whom we have no control over, but will also fail miserably in finding well deserved happiness within, if not focusing on what change is necessary within.

I most definitely understand that this change can be very difficult. For instance, it's not always easy to see the heavy impact of abuse when we are the one under constant attack. Physical and sexual abuse is more evident when taking place, but verbal and emotional abuse can be more easily disguised and therefore un-willingly or even unknowingly tolerated by the victim. Regardless of the type, victims of abuse each have many common traits. One significant trait is being trapped into believing "if I can just change, the abuser will change, and then the abusive circumstances will end." This false belief is sure to zap this person of any hope for joy. An abuser who does not want to be changed will never accept help from the one whom they are effortlessly scheming to keep stuck in a life of confusion and turmoil.

> *Repeat this scripture,* **"Faith is the substance of things hoped for and the evidence of things not seen." Hebrews 11:1**

Trying to fix someone else's problems takes a lot of our energy and usually, whether knowingly or not, becomes another avenue to avoid what we are not capable of fixing in our own life problems.

Rather than taking critical steps that can be a strong aid in sorting through what's keeping us stuck, we often become afraid and impatient. Being a typical reaction from many victims of abuse, once again we find ourselves relying on shortcuts to temporarily bring us comfort. These shortcuts or our self-efforts such as those mentioned in chapter 10 can be destructive choices and result in finding ourselves stuck even deeper in those mud and mire filled ruts.

How do we avoid the shortcuts of self efforts when faced with situations that if not taking immediate action, put our survival at stake? There is truth that at times taking necessary action can help to avoid making irrational, unhealthy decisions that can be a crucial part of survival. There are also times when we feel forced to take steps that we would not have chosen if circumstances around us were different. As mentioned earlier, when in a true crisis people tend to act in irrational ways if convinced there is no where else to turn.

For those in a situation of being forced to make a choice to stay in any relationship with one who is abusive to you physically, sexually, emotionally, or mentally, please know that you are worth much more than to remain joined with one who refuses to resolve abusive issues when yours or others safety is in question. You are of great worth and value.

This may be the time to consistently begin offering daily you're most intentional and sincere prayers whom to seek spiritual guidance from that can provide you with solid direction. While seeking wisdom for appropriate steps to take, don't resist God's lead on taking immediate and necessary action if your safety is at risk. He will provide you a way out, if relying on Him.

> _____ *is the substance of things hoped for and the* _____ *of things not seen, Hebrews 11:1.*

Rather than trying harder to please those whose intentions are to rob you of knowing the very joy you were designed to experience, begin searching for what you have the power to change within yourself--and stop looking for change in hopes to harden those eggshells you've been walking on for too long while allowing someone else control over your emotions. If you don't know where to start, talk to someone trustworthy who can help assist you in making changes that will bring you to a place of hope and move you away from the abusive situation. Focus Ministries hotline 800-799-SAFE (7233), and other resources listed in the Rock Solid Resource page in the back of this book will assist you with appropriate steps in removing yourself from the abusive situations.

Faith is the evidence! When we lose faith--we lose self control!!

Having a crime committed against us can result in feelings of unwarranted mistrust and un-forgiveness toward ourselves to such a degree that our ability to function is less than desirable, at minimum. These harsh experiences can fill our souls with a multitude of emotions that consume us with anger, contempt for self or others, guilt, and even shame. The combination of these emotions can be so intense that it can lead to feelings of worthlessness and if left alone a loss of self-control. The results end in a means to compensate for the loss that took place during the times of those abusive crimes against us. There will be times that this means of compensation (self destructive patterns) are expressed only through underlying, hidden reactions. In other words, we are not always aware of our reactions from the stronghold these emotions have over us.

As reminded previously, these deep rooted issues (whether we have awareness or not) can and usually will leave a negative impact on nearly everything and everyone that has any meaningful ties in our lives. Particularly impacted are those who love us, and equally those we love the most.

You may have resorted to the belief that the only way to freedom from the chains that are binding you is to take your life in your own hands. Too many times these two scenarios--trauma and a search for a way out of this precious gift of life--go hand in hand. Ending your life is not an option to freedom; it is most destructive. The enemy is out to destroy. With great emphasis--PLEASE know that "YOU" are worth more than that. There is most definitely somewhere to turn.

If you are battling suicidal thoughts, a phone call needs to take place immediately to 911, your healthcare provider or hospital, and at the least a trusted pastor or friend. Please turn to the Rock Solid Resource help page at the end of this book for more information on assistance with this. *I pray these thoughts are not yours and if they are, I pray you will get help now!*

1. Use this time to take a step back from any irrational ways of thinking that have been racing through your mind. Replace that energy with prayer while in search for the best plan of action that will bring you hope for the future. Though not instantly, but with consistent efforts in taking the appropriate steps, you can work through this. Hope is waiting.

2. Continue to remind yourself what real faith is. And also, know that practicing it will never lead you to false hopes.

Our awesome God, the Prince of Peace, will use our prayers simultaneously, and collectively, to change not only our own hearts, but the hearts of others to accomplish what He desires for all.

Journey Notes

CHAPTER 16

HOPE DEFERRED BECOMES A TREE OF LIFE

In the last chapter the impact of unhealthy relationships were discussed. In this chapter we will look at relationships from a different angle.

A traumatic experience can be a sure recipe for the enemy to successfully sever healthy relationships. When we are no longer capable of disguising the load we have been carrying from our past, there is a tendency to want to slowly tear down the bridges that connected us to those once strong, healthy relationships that might unmask more about our past than we are willing to give privilege to. In a sense, making that separation will help us not to have reminders from others who now are aware of the mess we have become, and then we can more easily avoid the brokenness that lies deep below that mess. Remember the out of sight, out of mind approach mentioned in chapter one? This tendency to believe it would be healthier to cut ties with those who otherwise would be safe for us to turn to when in need of support, if not careful, can block our healing process; keeping us stuck and delaying us from moving forward as we most deserve. The caution here is realizing that our contentment with believing that our situation will never change can become our best friend. There is nothing healthy in that false belief.

I'd like to take a look at this from another view. Perhaps temporarily separating yourself from some whom you have been dependent on for complete direction, could be necessary to move you into a stronger step of faith. In other words, this separation could be a *Devine* opportunity to permit God to show up in ways that otherwise you would have not been open to when in your most comfortable and familiar environment. While you will need to continue to have support, God can work best when all interferences (even those that are seemingly safe) step out of the way and let Him do His work. And when you are completely ready to rely on nothing more than His provisions, in His perfect timing you can be sure to watch how He will have someone lined up to walk along-side you with a fresh start. While absent of all obstacles that cause you to shut down in fear, you can find new hope in His guidance that will help you walk through that mess you have found yourself to become.

This *Divine* intervention (your appointed mentor) that was selected to walk with you may only be for a short while in order to place our focus back on Him, trusting only Him to be that direct link to our healing process and helping us to understand the hurt that caused us to feel more content if alone. With time, what we can only hope for can become great strength to us. It can be our tree of life if having enough faith to place our trust in the Lord to provide what we need at the exact time we need it.

> **Hopelessness leads to fears and fears lead to disobedience--patterns of destruction. *Hope deferred depresses, it makes the heart sick. But the fulfillment of hope strengthens our faith.... and when it comes we can trust it is a tree of life--Proverbs 13:12.***

So, when will you begin trusting in this process and have faith that God is using this time of temporary isolation to bring restoration in your life?

When hopelessness sneaks in, permit yourself to seek guidance, as there could be times when spiritual counsel from another may be necessary, and acceptable, on your path to recovery. We tend to be weary of this for various reasons. For some it's a trust issue, "How can anyone possibly understand what I am going through, or care enough to want to continue to walk with me when the most intricate details begin to unfold?" Others may struggle with the fact that the issues they are dealing with are not severe enough to constitute a need for someone else to help them sort through the details of their difficulties.

Another common take on resisting necessary support is, "Everyone has problems, only those who can't handle life need help from another." Getting caught up in any of these forms of denial will only keep one comfortably stuck in the ruts of mud and mire. Again, if not careful, contentment becomes our best friend. In times of desperation we can be more easily steered toward the alternative of self-help that leaves us with nothing solid to stand on when the raging waters once again begin consuming our emotions.

Those of us who are believers sometimes have a different level of difficulty with fear of turning to someone for counsel. The idea of needing someone to walk alongside them through their difficulties, to this person, means they are not fully trusting God. Their belief system is that only God can offer adequate hope for change, so to them turning to a counselor for help means turning away from God. When prayerfully seeking spiritual counsel to walk with us through the paths of recovery, trust in knowing that we can still remain committed to God's word, and not worldly views, for sufficient guidance.

There is such great power in prayer: Pray now for wisdom from God to send you to the one He has lined up to be "Jesus in the flesh" for your appointed time to properly heal.

Pray to avoid seeking out someone who is giving advice based on worldly views that will only add to any destructive patterns your heart now desires to overcome.

You will know the difference when what you hear lines up with God's word--His book of instructions. This book carries a vast amount of guidance that points us to a path of joy, purpose, and great worth. Through this you will discover the success in your search to understand that through prayer and scripture reading His Word will point you toward meaningful counsel and guidance.

Pray for wisdom and discernment to know His Word as you obediently remain in His Word. Then, wait patiently for God's direction to unfold as He honors your obedience.

I WAITED PATIENTLY ON THE LORD...................

It will take patience to completely commit to letting go of your own self-desires and submit to His guidance. This is not a natural thing to do for most; still it is not impossible with God's guidance. Remember; steer away from the shortcuts that cause you to fall back into that rut of being stuck in the false hope that change can never take place.

While walking through the discomfort of these steps put your focus on things from above and then be willing to patiently watch what God is doing as you begin to experience an awesome transformation of the heart. Patience will increase as you continue to grow accustom to the smoothness of this path, relieving you from eruptions of chaos that you once knew on your endless journey of self-help.

HE SET MY FEET ON A ROCK AND GAVE ME A FIRM PLACE TO STAND...............................

Grace has a way of turning everything that's upside down, inside out, by turning it outward from self and into God's care.

When we see that God's shoulders are much bigger than ours and His arm is not too short to reach out and hold us up, our understanding becomes greater in learning how to let go of our battles and let Him fight them for us. While He is fighting, He is preparing us for the battle of healing and recovery. The results are beautiful; a true and lasting peace in our lives. Our hearts were wired to desire this. In order to maintain this beautiful relationship we have to not only believe in the source that can provide this, but rely fully on the source that will never fail this. You will know this to be true when you discover that the source you turn to for refuge will certainly never again attempt to *convince you that things can never change.*

1. What source are you currently relying on when in need of refuge? Take the time now to write out what you have turned to in the past in hopes to find change.

2. What were the results?

3. Later did you find yourself repeating the same patterns of feeling you were drowning in chaos—-or did you feel a constant flow of peace that this source remained rock solid while holding you up until the raging waters had descended?

   Why or why not?

God does not expect perfection; He only expects obedience. Through our obedience He can and will turn our failures into His triumphs.

Remember where disobedience takes us: farther than you ever want to go and will cost you more than you ever want to pay. It's up to you to decide how long you want to stay in disobedience. What will your choice be?

> *God is our strength and refuge,*
> *An ever present help in times of trouble.*
> *Therefore we will not fear,*
> *Though the earth gives way and the*
> *mountains fall into the sea.*
> *Though the waters roar and foam and the*
> *mountains quake with their surging....He will*
> *provide strength and a refuge. Psalm 46:1-4*

Again, it's a heart change that brings the healing necessary to remove any chains that keep us bound in the dissatisfaction, hopelessness, and the false belief that whatever we are struggling with can never change. Intentional prayer can transfer what remains stuck in our minds over to a beautiful transformation of our hearts. Remember that our hearts are the compartment that allows Jesus to mold us and mend our brokenness. Our hearts are a safe compartment that the enemy can never gain access to when giving in to the Prince of Peace, who "will" provide true and lasting peace in our lives when relying on Him.

He is rock solid, even when the earth gives way and mountains fall into the seas. He is rock solid, even when the seas roar and foam. He is rock solid, even when the mountains begin their quaking!

> *Be still and know that I am God....Psalm 46:10.*

4. What needs to change in order for you to make solid choices that will enable you to trust in traveling a secure and smooth path in your future?

I waited patiently on the Lord; He turned to me and heard my cry. He lifted me out of the slimy pit, out of the mud and mire; He set my feet on a rock and gave me a firm place to stand. He put a new song in my mouth, a hymn of praise to our God. Many will see and fear and put their trust in the Lord. Blessed is the man who puts their trust in the Lord...Psalm 40:1-4

No circumstance, past or present, can ever remove this truth.

No circumstance, past or present, can ever separate us from His love.

HIS LOVE IS ROCK SOLID!!

Journey Notes

CHAPTER 17

AM I WORTH IT?

While reminding me of Biblical truths, a very compassionate friend, George Stahnke, founder of Renewal Ministries of Colorado Springs, shared these words, "You are a woman of worth and value, cherished and loved by God." Having never heard these words spoken to me before, it left me speechless. These few words held such POWER that I could neither deny it nor believe it. I spent the next few days processing this powerful statement, much of that time questioning whether or not this statement could hold truth and meaning to my own personal life. Over time, God began revealing to me that His unconditional love, His great mercy, and His never ending grace offered just that--truth and meaning to anyone who would receive it, even me.

George was used as a tool to provide me with rock solid counsel at the appointed time. Still it was God's Word, not his, that convicted me to know how valuable my life is, and how deeply my Lord and Savior does love and cherish me. I have since been learning to separate the feelings of holding little value to others from the security in knowing that my greatest reward is to believe that God continuously holds me close, while filling the gap for my need of comfort through others.

Nothing else has ever been of greater comfort to me than knowing this **"There is no greater love than to lay down one's life for others".
John 15:13**

No matter where we came from, what we have done, or how broken we may become, each of us holds an enormous amount of worth and value and is unconditionally loved and cherished by God. He yearns for us to see this. He yearns for us to feel this. And, when we believe that this powerful statement stands true in our personal lives, we can begin living it out in such a way that we cannot wait to share this truth with others.

Deliverance is freedom: no longer repeating that cycle that lead to patterns of destruction.

Being set free from the chains that once held you in bondage allows the freedom for deliverance to begin. At that point we can more easily recognize that all shame and guilt we carry can be replaced with worth and value. As self-worth and value begin to penetrate within our hearts, moving us closer to what God created us to be, it also begins to peel away each layer of pain, leaving the past as only memories. Memories are now reminders of how God has taken something once so heavy and transformed it into something absolutely beautiful. To our amazement, we find ourselves praising God for allowing us to endure those heavy times long enough to understand that, even in the midst of those hardships, a plan was being laid for a glorious ending.

Even when we believe the circumstances around us can only leave us victim, God's plan for our lives is victory. We are never alone. Our trials which had once convinced us were only good for keeping us in bondage, are now loosened chains, ringing with freedom.

In Philippians chapter 1 verse 12, Paul writes his desire for others to understand that the trials which he experienced took place for the spreading of the gospel. While taking a stand for what matters the most, (sharing the Love of Jesus) Paul chose to endure suffering in order to keep a commitment to the calling of God's unique plan to use him. It would seem apparent to most folks that imprisonment would zap any desires for ministering. Yet Paul remained obedient, he never lost sight of ministering to others even at the cost of his life. He was used by God to provide strong spiritual counsel--Jesus in the flesh.

1. In what are you seeking for refuge and strength?

2. When reality sets in that you alone are not adequate to provide the desired refuge and strength in your most difficult times, where or what do you turn to?

3. Do you find yourself working tirelessly to try and prove to yourself of having value and worth in your life? This could look like many things: replacing the pain with self-efforts or such worldly things as described in chapter 10.

   Refer back to chapter 10 if needed and then test this by truthfully answering the following questions.

4. Are you hiding behind a mask, and living out a life of pretense, so that all who see will not be allowed to know of the less attractive stories in your life's book; the visions that keep you stuck in pain?

5. Do you find yourself pouring your energy into trying to control and fix broken things in hopes of erasing the visions that keep you stuck in pain?

6. Or, are you able to confront the truth and stand firm in claiming, "If I can't erase this vision, then I choose to replace this vision with love and grace so that the past will no longer be remembered as pain, and instead be used as gain?"

7. Write what thoughts come to your mind when thinking about gaining from your pain. Do you think that is possible? Why or why not?

Take time now to reflect on your reaction to these questions. You may have to go back and read them again in order to process what this means to you.

With strong emphasis, I urge you to write out these thoughts now so later you can measure how your immediate reaction may lead you to "take" action and no longer sit idle in those consuming thoughts. I am hopeful you will trust the process even if it does not make sense now.

When we embrace love and grace as a replacement for heartache and shame we are gradually able to loosen the ties of our mask. Then, when least expected, this mask that was once worn to cover the less attractive stories in a secret dark place locked within the pit of our souls--a place where we thought only we could hold the key--will soon begin to fall off.

God's love and grace requires no forced entrance to unlock our deepest secrets.

He only requires us to trust that when His love covers our pain, then His grace will replace our shame. The freedom that comes with this is so great that the lock we had on our deepest secrets begins to slip away. No forced entry! God's love and grace are the real keys to effectively unlock the compartment that once kept us in a cycle of destructive patterns. The key has been revealed; we have passed the test. We no longer have the need to be perfect, just obedient.

Though the earth gives way and the mountains fall into the sea, we are free of fear because the author of love, God, is our strength and refuge, "our solid rock" and an ever present help when times of trouble come our way. God's love is so great and awesome!!! God's love is Rock Solid!

When we can trust in this, no longer will the enemy have hold on the memories that consumed our lives with fear. No longer will the enemy have a place in the deep parts of our soul where those silent, dark memories once remained hidden.

8. What is it that you really want to trust in but continue to replace with a strong desire of self-efforts?

Journey Notes

CHAPTER 18

BREAKING THE CHAINS

This chapter will help us relate to how we can find victory in breaking free from chains that keep us enslaved to our old destructive patterns. I'd like to invite you to first read about Paul's journey found in Acts chapter 9 verses 1-31. Then, read the first chapter in Philippians and chapter 2, verses 1-11 also in Philippians. This reading will help in understanding how we can be strengthened even when in bondage, no matter our circumstances.

For taking a stand for what really matters, Paul chose to endure suffering. Yet he remained obedient, Paul never lost sight of ministering. We should be reminded that he also was once an unbeliever in Christ. His only mission was to persecute those who openly expressed their love and obedience for the One whose love was unconditional for all. Even a confessed murderer, such as Paul, could break free from those chains that kept him bound in dissatisfaction, hopelessness, and false beliefs that the darkness in his life would ever change.

Maybe you can relate to someone like Paul and his poor choices in life before God gave him a new meaning and purpose of sharing Christ's unconditional love, rather than keeping him stuck in false beliefs in the midst of his sufferings. Perhaps you've suffered from poor choices in the past or more recently. When we see that even a heart filled with murderous consent can be changed and restored to a life of fullness, is that not enough to empower us to believe that whatever struggles we have encountered can be delivered? On the other hand, whatever sins we have committed can and will be forgiven?

Or maybe you can better relate to someone like Paul when he was held in bondage while in prison. While his only accusation was sharing the love of Jesus, no crime was committed. Paul did nothing to deserve imprisonment. He was a victim of others hard heartedness, calloused minds, and who find joy in pleasing selfish needs while robbing others of theirs.

God will give you the patience and the ability to rise above what is meant for destruction in yours and others lives around you, even when enticed by the enemy's dangerous grip. Be prepared, because you may even find that God has chosen to use your new found understanding of personal struggles! He can use this understanding to move you alongside others to help them through their walk of darkness in their own struggles, just as He did in Paul's life even while imprisoned. There is a difference between being stuck in painful memories and remembering what brought on your pain. During your healing you may find yourself asking, "Lord, why won't you remove these painful memories of my past?" Don't be surprised when He replies something like this, "My precious child, I don't want you to forget. I need you to give me your complete trust and then believe that the fullness of your healing will come, as I prepare you to share with others. It's through those painful memories that will bring you to the understanding that I was there all along and a greater understanding of what I have done for you.

This is the part of the process when the pain begins peeling away--one layer at a time. As obedience takes place and we become open to God's purpose for our personal dark experiences, we find ourselves wanting to share our deliverance from the strong chains that once held us captive. A clearer sight of a smoother path is now ahead! This path reveals God's purpose for the struggles for which others had also once believed they would never find hope for healing.

1. Do you find yourself working hard to try and prove to yourself of having value and worth in your life?

2. When looking back over the questions at the end of chapter 15, what, if any, masks did you discover you could be hiding behind that prevent you from allowing the awesomeness of God's grace and love to replace the visions that keep you stuck in what was unpleasant in your past?

3. What mask are you now discovering?

4. Did you take time out to reflect on your reaction to those questions in chapter 15? Go back and read what you wrote. Perhaps you didn't have anything to put into words at that time. If so, why do you think the words would not come?

5. Do you need to be more honest about anything at this point? Don't rush, this is your time to rest in God's love and grace and pour out any thoughts that keep you stuck in false beliefs of having no worth or value.

Even if you are not ready to believe this go ahead and speak these truths, "If I can't erase this vision, then I choose to replace this vision with love and grace so that the past will no longer be remembered as pain, and instead be used as gain.

Repeat it again. "If I can't erase this vision, then I choose to replace this vision with love and grace so that the past will no longer be remembered as pain, and instead be used as gain."

Now feel free to write whatever it is that's racing through your mind. Remember, this is your time to rest in God's love and grace. This next page is reserved for you when you are ready to pour out these thoughts, perhaps for the first time, that keep you stuck in the false truths of believing you hold no worth or value. Don't be concerned about complete sentences, grammar, punctuation, etc... Remember God is not looking for perfection only obedience. Just write from the depths of your heart!

> **"I will be your strength and refuge - be still and know that I am God"**

Use the space on the following pages to pour your heart out to God:

Journey Notes

CHAPTER 19

"YOU" ARE WORTH IT!!

God deeply desires to deliver you from any destructive impact your victimization may attempt to bring. He will give you the patience and the ability to rise above what the enemy has planned for destruction in your life, and for how this destruction will impact others' lives' around you. Others around us are also affected by whether we choose to receive the Grace that only He has to offer to raise us above whatever the enemy is endlessly fighting to destroy. His desires and abilities to work through even our heaviest burdens are not meant to be kept to ourselves. Whether crimes committed against you or crimes committed by you (which many times will accompany the first), there is deliverance waiting.

Our loving God's plan is never intended for you to be ready to walk through the process of removing each layer of pain alone. He knows too well that the pain you have stored is through a multitude of events throughout your life. To gain your trust to lead you through it, He first has to gain your trust to let Him love you through it. This will require an adequate stretch of time for God to help you to be ready to discover complete freedom.

Pray for patience and endurance as He works you through the process.

This process will begin when you are ready for the pain to be transferred over to Him. It may seem to move slower than desired, as each layer removed needs ample time to heal before the next layer is strong enough to endure its own surgery. While working through each layer the hard stuff is eventually removed, calluses become thinner, and then transference to Him becomes easier. One day when least expecting you will discover a glimpse of your pain being lessoned.

The battle is almost over!

Through faithfulness and obedience, while allowing Him to carry you through the raging waters, doors of opportunity will begin to open for you. It's then that you find the amazing understanding that it was because of what you had once endured that another hurting soul may also discover the ability to be set free--only if you're willing to allow your obedience and the painfulness of past experiences to be used.

"But, I don't have time or energy to deal with the load others are carrying." This would be a normal response from many. This response is the reluctance of letting go of the weight of the baggage in your own life that is still fresh. A strong reminder is that the same healing power which you once thought could never occur in your own life can now be bearing witness to others as you begin to live your life out loud. Living out loud may be an uncomfortable place at first, but will eventually move you to discovering more beautiful places. Places which you never thought could be possible for you.

There is truth that there is such great purpose for you. Through patience and trust you will find that the final layers of pain are removed--God will begin using this pain as gain. This is perhaps the final stage to the beginning of your purpose for enduring those unpleasant experiences. Your purpose is now being lived out loud through great deliverance. This, friend, is huge; deliverance is your heart's desire.

Be still and know that I am God.....

1. What will it take for you to begin your healing process? YOU ARE WORTH IT!!

Journey Notes

CHAPTER 20

THE TRUTH WILL SET YOU FREE

How will your story end? What will you testify to? How will the purpose of the stories in your life's book be used? I can testify that God loves you too much to allow your pain to be wasted. Maybe it's time for you to begin working through those final layers, begin finding your joy, purpose and worth through bearing witness to another soul also in need of deliverance. Embrace God's awesome love that's fighting for you to unfriend bitterness with your past.

Restoration from past issues may not always come in a way that line up to our level of understanding or expectations of moving forward. Yearning for restoration from damages that occurred over time may very well aide to one's burdened heart of life long bitterness, if that yearning heart never allows God to guide us to a brokenness that will truly set us free. The damages you have suffered are real, but are not beyond repair.

If this were true, Jesus' death on the cross would be for naught. His sufferings were real yet there was great hope while enduring what would appear to be un-repairable damages to the many who witnessed his suffering on the cross, and then His resurrection to life. Jesus, being God in the human flesh, could have chosen to escape from carrying the burden He would face on the cross. Still, He kept His sight on things above, while believing His pain and suffering would be temporary and not wasted, rather, would be used to bring a hope of light and life to all that was once hidden by darkness. His sacrifice continues to bring hope to all who will receive it today. It is the same now as it was then.

As we walk through the initial steps of healing we can understand that full relief is absent without going to the next level of truths. Our deepest healing comes from the truths in repentance. Repentance is not self pity, self contempt, or even sorrow for wrong doing. Repentance is to turn away and look the opposite direction, therefore changing our hearts and minds. What does this mean for those who have suffered deeply through circumstances they had no control over?

If you have been this victim, please know that you are not to blame for innocent suffering brought upon you. The repentance spoken of here is about being set free from the false truths we have chosen to live under while believing our worth and value was dependent on and determined by these circumstances that caused our suffering. The only wrong doing here is believing in those false truths. Your worth and value is not determined by your past or your present circumstances. Your past does not define your worth and value in Christ.

> ### *If you repent I will restore you that you may serve me. Jeremiah 15:19*

You are a woman/man of worth and value, cherished and loved by God. Continue to remind yourself of the Gift. You are a woman/man of worth and value, cherished and loved by God. I _____, have worth and value. I _____ am cherished and loved by God. YOUR NAME BELONGS HERE!

You can rest in knowing that this truth does apply to you too. When you are ready to place your name on these lines be prepared to experience repentance. When no more living in the darkness of false truths, you are now accepting Jesus' gift to all, so that you may live complete in His forgiveness.

What greater gift than to give ones life for another.

Be prepared as well, that when you receive this gift you'll experience, in full color, how your pain and suffering will not be wasted. But it will be used to bring a light of hope in the life of others, just as Jesus' example was used for us through His pain and sufferings.

> *By His stripes you have been healed 1 Peter 2:24*

Then, lastly, be prepared to believe that you are not exempt from this gift. These are passages to help you in your healing from destructive patterns and then lead you to truths in experiencing the freedom of glorious recovery. Your chains are gone--you've been set free.

> *The truth will set you free. John 8:32.*

When receiving forgiveness toward ourselves, then believing we too can be a tool to bring light to another's life that was once hidden in darkness, we find that our own pain and suffering becomes only temporary. True repentance will move us from bitterness into forgiveness. Forgiveness offers us freedom. There is evidence in truth that your past does not define your worth and value in Christ; just as there is evidence in truth that His sacrifice for you on the cross will surely set you free.

Bitterness?

Unforgiveness?

Suffering?

Pain?

Self-pity?

Self-contempt?

Victimization?

Ambivalence?

There are surely many thoughts rushing through your mind right now.

1. Which of these emotions is too heavy for you to continue to own? This is a good time to lay them out before the Lord.

Don't hold them back; He can handle it.... if there is something heavy on your mind release it here in this safe place. Whatever it is--you deserve to be set free from these emotions.

2. What does your heart desire to feel right now?

Freedom?

Clarity?

Hope?

Relief?

Joy?

A life of purpose?

Worth and value?

Loved?

If the son sets you free, then you are truly free. John 8:36

Journey Notes

CHAPTER 21

WHERE DO I START?

> *The Lord lives! Praise be to my Rock - Psalm 18:46*

Eventually you will come to the safe place of knowing you are no longer holding yourself or others responsible for keeping you bound in chains. Self-contempt is now replaced with focusing on how to begin to live your life out loud in truth, despite the choices others make. It's not perfection but obedience that frees us from the cycle of destructive patterns we mistakenly choose when life's storms take place.

Look over the "Journey Notes" and the questions which you struggled answering in the previous chapters. Spend some time now revisiting your thoughts to those questions.

1. What are you feeling at this moment about what you were unable to express at that time?

2. What emotions have since surfaced that need to be validated at this time which you were unable to process previously? It's okay to add or change any new emotions you have discovered. These are the truths you are searching for throughout your journey.

It may take some time to put a name to your emotions and have the ability to speak them out honestly. Don't be alarmed to find in the beginning steps of taking charge of your emotions that you may be expressing them with much discomfort and in anger, especially if you have never been privileged to communicate your true thoughts before now. The truth is that your feelings and thoughts really do matter! You deserve to feel the way you feel. This is simply the expression of your pain's desire to be released and will lesson as you come to accept that you are safe in doing so. So be patient!

When the emotions of pain begin to surface, allow yourself to not only feel this pain, but also to journey into what has caused the pain--put a name on it. The old tendencies in your past would be to never allow yourself to experience the emotions of pain brought on by bitterness, anger, or even resentment from your past offenders. What you were taught was to adhere to someone else's needs and hold back expressing your own needs. There is no deliverance in this choice--only destruction!

It's important to be reminded that regurgitation is neither pretty nor comfortable for any of us, but with practice, know that a transformation can take place as this pain begins to be replaced with something more beautiful. A transformation of love and grace will begin to fill the gaps and move you toward living your life out loud in truth, and not in bitter pain as you learn to express your needs to others. Whether or not they accept this is their responsibility. Continue to practice these new feelings--the words that you so desire to express in love and grace will get easier!

Now that we see how God desperately wants to work through our pain, what do we do with it? We don't have to look long and hard to discover that others have faced similar challenges in their lives. It's easy for us to believe we are the only ones that could ever experience these areas of struggles. Part of healing is knowing you are not alone!

In the beginning pages I pointed out that many of us have a story and a testimony of how God showed up at a time of desperation for refuge and something solid to rest on. How easy it would be to share in testimony what God is doing through our own lives to others who have not yet embraced the truths which we have now been privileged to understand. Pray about how God will use your pain as gain in someone else's life. Watch as He opens the doors of opportunity to finally share your witness with one you have been praying for. And, don't be surprised when these same doors open to share your witness with someone who un-expectantly crosses your path.

Scripture tells us that God does not comfort us just to make ourselves comfortable; rather, **God comforts us so *that we can become comforters for others, 2 Corinthians 1: 3, 4.***

Because of the truth in this passage, you can be certain to know that He strongly desires to use your pain as gain.

Keep practicing!

Journey Notes

CHAPTER 22

SPEAK SOLID TRUTH IN LOVE

> *Though my father and mother forsake me,*
> *the Lord will receive me. Psalm 27:10.*

This chapter is devoted to the truths of the life long impact for those whose lives have been psychologically wounded by the broken relationship of a parent. I will focus more particularly on fathers, since it is more common for this role to be absent. You will be able to apply the same information covered in this chapter even if your own situation relates better to the role of an absent mother.

I believe that to know the love of a father is to know a love that has a *positive* and lasting impact on one's life--one that nothing else could *ever* replace. I also believe, in contrast, that living a life *without* knowing the love of a father can leave a lasting *negative* impact on one's life. The good news is that *this negative impact can most definitely* be replaced, once we allow our wounded hearts to be led to a place of discovery that, even to the fatherless, the embracing arms of a father's love do not have to remain absent.

There is a love that is unconditional, one that never gives up on us no matter the circumstances surrounding us. This, known as agape love, is never based on our circumstances, rather is completely unconditional toward our actions and abilities.

Practicing the destructive patterns described throughout the previous chapters may only be one's reaction to never having known this kind of love. Men and women, who have not experienced a nurturing relationship that was originally designed for us to have with a parent, will usually feel unworthy of this love. Harboring unhealthy feelings toward ourselves that lead to the destructive patterns named throughout this book, often times is a result of unhealthy relationships with those we were so wonderfully, uniquely, and intimately created to interact with the most. The removal of this interaction from one's life leaves a gap in our hearts that can make it difficult to wrap our minds around to know how to follow that design He intentionally knitted within us. So, how do we then honor our father and mother as God commanded?

Some will find that being obedient to this command will not bring about the healthy return hoped for. While there is the possibility that rejection may shatter what is hoped to achieve in your efforts of obedience to God's commands, it should not change our choice to act out what we are instructed by our Divine Creator. A question I have learned to ask is, "Is my heart in the right place in order to practice this command?" If the answer is no, then I have to decide whether I will choose to take ownership of that, or live my life out in discord. The discord I am speaking of is the weight of emotional and psychological confusion within. Ultimately, those in close relationships with us (such as a spouse, children or friends) will also be strongly impacted by any consequences from this emotional confusion which only aids in the continuous cycle of destruction in our lives.

We should be mindful that being obedient to what God calls us to do is not only meant to benefit ourselves. I believe that the fifth commandment always stands to be true--even if the only thing you get in return is rejection in your attempts to remain obedient.

> *Exodus 12:15 tells us this,* **"Honor your father and mother so that you may live long in the land your God is giving to you."**

God's Grace does have a way of turning us inside out. Obedience is only witnessed on the outside if and when honor takes place on the inside. Transformation of our hearts changes what is needed on the inside so that the results can be witnessed by others through our actions on the outside; this heart change now shows evidence in our actions.

Regardless of the indications of my unpleasant childhood memories mentioned in the beginning chapters, I want to close with these final chapters revealing a significant discovery which I hope will leave an even stronger lasting impact on you-- a discovery that is being echoed throughout this book. A discovery that will help you to clearly understand you *are* of great worth and value and greatly cherished and loved by God.

In chapter four I mentioned that my relationship with my earthly father had found a new level of growth during his last days spent with us. But only through the greatness of my heavenly father's agape love have I had the ability to discover the "fight" in me to want what I never fully knew existed before now.

The strong control in just three words, "I love you," can be such a powerful force in how our lives are lived out.

The path I eventually chose to take in my journey after much time in search for truth is what empowered me to not be consumed by the absence of those words throughout my life. Those three words were only recently spoken to me from my father's now frail voice for the first time.

In the recent years I had begun acting in boldness by continuously expressing my love to him with full awareness that there would be no response in return. Then recently, I made the decision that if I were to ever know how he genuinely felt about me, I would have to ask. While

I can't share that my father stepped up to initiate nor freely offer his confirmation of love for me, I still received those three words with a huge amount of peace. And I truly do believe I witnessed great peace in him when he finally gave in and honored my last request before he died, which I have to believe in turn honored his.

I am now so very grateful that through this part of my journey, I have discovered the ability to more fully understand the realness of love from my *heavenly* father, despite the barriers surrounding me throughout the many years of not being privileged of feeling the warm embrace of my *earthly* father's love. Finally, while standing beside him as he took his last breath, it suddenly became clearer to me that during all those years perhaps my earthly father only had the ability to express his love for his children in the only way he was taught to offer it.

The fifty years it took to say "I love you" was my father's own journey... and an unspoken testimony when he finally shared his faith in the saving grace of God's son Jesus, never spoken until those final days.

Because I chose to take those critical steps through my personal journey described in this book, I can now testify that God's grace has a way of turning us inside out. There is great freedom in finding God's love in areas I thought would never be possible. The key to unlocking those deep secrets within my heart was finally revealed to me through love, grace, and mercy that only come from above.

Agape love is not circumstantial; rather it flows from giving of the same grace and mercy that I do not deserve. Not only is it freely given to me if I choose to receive it, I can choose to freely pass this on to others. The same amount of grace that God offers to us, even when we do not seemingly deserve it, is just as worthy of being passed on to others, whom at times we believe cannot be justified if doing so. It may not seem fair; still, it is always justified when we are reminded of the love that took place on the cross.

This kind of love will never have to be asked for!

The truth is that many will not be given the opportunity from their earthly father to find peace with them, no matter how much they desire this. I know others personally who are extremely desperate for this peace, and no matter how hard they try to achieve it, only find rejection. If this is you, know that you too have the choice to replace this rejection with something else that can cleanse your polluted heart, free you from the heavy weight of these chains, and lead to a positively beautiful outcome.

It may take much effort and a whole new level of understanding of what it really means to trust before the discovery is made that YOU do have a choice to find the ability of discovering this beautiful outcome. We may have to keep reminding ourselves over again that Jesus' gift to each of us on the cross was not fair. Still, it was justified then and is so as strongly now. Even today, He chooses to accept those of us whom others have rejected. What a discovery! God, my daddy, sees me as a woman of great worth and value regardless of my circumstances. I know I am cherished and loved by Him.

It's time to no longer rely on your past or present circumstances in finding the life of peace you desire and deserve--you won't find it there.

You have a choice!

Wait for the Lord; Be strong, take heart and wait for the Lord. He will be your strength and refuge in times of trouble. An ever present help. There is no need to fear, though the earth gives, the mountains fall into the sea, though its waters roar and foam and the mountains quake with their surging. There is a river whose streams make glad the city of God, the holy place where the Most High dwells. God is within her, she will not fall. God will help her at the break of day. Be still and know that you will find what you are looking for in God. *Psalm 27:14 & 46: 1-5, 10*

---

1. If you have found that place of peace in a broken relationship with a parent, then stop now and praise God for walking alongside you in your much needed time for strength and refuge. Praise Him for equipping you to choose to practice those steps which your journey has brought you to.

2. If you are waiting for this relationship to be mended, patiently continue to pray for God to bring you peace in knowing that He will fill the gaps of that brokenness.

Journey Notes

CHAPTER 23

EXODUS: THE JOURNEY OUT

One last choice you can make before laying this book aside is to commit to a new life of truth in scripture reading and prayer time with God. When you take the time daily to speak to Him, He will take time daily to guide you on a smooth path that will keep you from falling back into a rut of turning to those cycles of destructive patterns when life's storms take place once again. Challenge yourself to begin regularly spending time with God daily for the next two weeks. Use the final pages of this book to journal your prayers each day for two weeks before you start any routines, whether its house work, a public job, or family obligations. After you have prayed, listen for God's still small voice and begin searching for understanding in how He is working you through your recovery and healing by going to His word. I have learned it is also helpful to write down what He reveals to me through my prayer time when requesting God to give me the exact passages to read that will aid in bringing life to my communication with Him.

Through daily prayer journaling, God can strongly remind you of where you once were and where He has now brought you to in your journey. When you come to the point that you are able to compare the distance between the two, is when your road to victory is claimed! You are then released from the false beliefs of being a victim.

The battle is won!

Giving your time to Him first will fill in those ruts that tend to keep you stuck in the destructive patterns you now find possible to escape. The results of starting your day in His word pave a much smoother path throughout your day. Don't forget where you were and don't be surprised to see where this commitment of routine prayer and scripture reading will take you as you begin to practice it daily. Something worth praying about during your two week commitment:

Pray – through prayer you are allowing yourself to acknowledge that you no longer have to carry your heavy burdens alone. This is a good place to begin letting go of the heavy weight that keeps you stuck in the false belief that change can never take place.

Acknowledge – that there is someone who knows your great worth and value. Acknowledge that someone knows your inner thoughts, see your every fault, and still invites you to be bathed in His unceasing love.

Acknowledgement is one step closer to letting go of the pain that hinders us from living our lives out loud in truth.

Pray – that you will embrace the comfort that's waiting for you and not resist it. Pray that you can continue to acknowledge that your strength alone is not enough to keep you on that smooth path when life's storms begin to rage.

Repent – turn away from anything that keeps you from living your life out loud in these truths. When you find yourself falling back onto an uneven path that brings about false beliefs you were once accustomed to, pray even louder for continued resistance. Remember where you once were during that smooth path of living your life out loud.

Pray – for your heart and mind to be changed toward those who have caused you pain and then pray for deliverance for any wrong doing in your own life.

Choose – to live your life out loud in truth. Choose to know that you were worth dying for. Choose to be freed from the false belief that change can never occur in your life. Choose to respond in love (and with appropriate boundaries) to those who are your enemies, regardless of their choices.

Pray – that you will not define the worth and value of your life by your past or present circumstances. Rather embrace knowing that your worth and value are defined in Christ's love for you when He buried your burdens on the cross.

Forgive – allow your bitterness to be buried by His forgiveness. Forgive not only others, but forgive yourself as Christ has forgiven you.

Pray - never ceasing for wisdom and strength to acknowledge God's truths, repent from wrong doing toward others and self; choose to live your life out loud through His love and grace daily; and allow God's healing power to turn bitterness into sweet forgiveness.

Christ wants to equip us with His truths so that we don't have to understand the things in life that make no sense to us. Regardless of whether the stuff that has filled your life with baggage fits the categories mentioned throughout these pages or derive from other areas, you can know a life of rock solid passages to recovery that ***surpasses all understanding by guarding your hearts and minds in Christ Jesus – Philippians 4:7***

Know that you can replace those chains that continue to keep you bound in false truths with believing that God will meet your every need when walking daily in ROCK SOLID--PASSAGES TO RECOVERY.

Be still and know that I am God!!

Document how you will begin to "Live your Life out Loud"

1. Write about what God revealed to you during this time of self study-

2. What changes need to take place in order for you to live your life out loud the way you were created?

Begin documenting them while it is fresh on your mind

....Begin your two week 'Prayer Journal' here:
Day 1

Day 2

Day 3

Day 4

Day 5

Day 6

Day 7

Day 8

Day 9

Day 10

Day 11

Day 12

Day 13

Day 14

You have just spent the past two weeks sharing your most intimate thoughts with the one most intimate relationship you will ever know.... Jesus!

The first words of this book began with this simple, yet all encompassing truth: GOD IS SO GOOD! For many who have gone through a painful past discovering truths in God's great love, grace, and mercy does not come without much hard work! I commend you for taking these steps....that's the natural process of healing! You too can discover these truths by choosing His Son Jesus Christ for refuge and strength that is always present in times of trouble when we call on His name.

I want to take this last moment to emphasize that choosing the pain of emotional surgery *WILL* replace what had once polluted your heart and move you toward healing and a positive future when also choosing to place it in the loving arms of Christ!

Stay the course--you are worth it!

Continue to not only believe in this truth, but continue to receive this truth.

Communication with God through daily prayer, Bible reading, and journaling will keep you on a smooth path. Reading back over your journals of your journey will help you to remember where you once were and to more clearly see where you are now headed. Prayer and Bible reading will give you strength to continue through your healing process.

Thank you for allowing me to join you in your journey of trusting God. Let me be the first to congratulate you on embracing His guidance through your passages to recovery that are now **"Rock Solid".**

ROCK SOLID RESOURCES

Suicidal Ideation:

If you are having immediate thoughts of harming yourself or someone else call 911 now!

Telling a friend, family member or co-worker can be a great amount of support in holding you accountable to remain committed to getting help, regardless of what path you take in getting help!

If you feel safe in that you are able to control these emotions during this time there is still a need to contact a professional who can help you to work through these thoughts in the safest way possible. The following suggested contacts are listed in the order of priority that can be most beneficial to providing you the immediate help you deserve.

1. Your physician knows your history better than anyone and can be the most beneficial to guiding you to someone who best fits your needs.
2. If for some reason you are not comfortable with talking to your physician, contact your pastor, or one at a local church if you do not have a pastor at this time.
3. The following are available resources that can guide you to find a professional in your community that can meet your immediate need.

   *American Association of Christian Counselors - provides referrals for local professional Christian Counselors nearest you. Website www.aacc.net - phone: 1-800-526-8673

*Focus on the Family - provides referrals for local professional Christian Counselors nearest you. Website: www.focusonthefamily.com - phone: 1-800-A-Family

*Teen Rescue USA - provides Christ based locations for teens in need of extensive crisis counseling for dealing with life controlling issues. Website: www.teenrescueusa/hotline - phone: 1-800-SUICIDE / 1-800-784-2433 / or 1-800-273-TALK / 1-800-273-8255 / 1-800-779-4TTY / 1-800-779-4889 call 24/7

Books:

Suicide Prevention: author June Hunt - When life seems hopeless. www.Christianbooks.com

Too Soon to Say Goodbye: - authors Susan Titus Osborn, Karen L Kosman, Jeenie Gordon - Healing and Hope for Victims and Survivors of Suicide - www.Christianbooks.com

Abuse - emotional, physical, sexual, and verbal:

FOCUS Ministries - is a not-for-profit 501(c) 3 organization offering hope, encouragement, support, education, spiritual direction, and assistance to teens, women, and families who experience domestic violence, destructive relationships, separation, or divorce email: help@foucministries1.org / www.focusministries1.org

Safe People - Authors Henry Cloud and John Townsend Countless individuals have invested themselves into people who've shipwrecked their lives in return. They've lost the sense of security and personal value in the process. If you're one who has chosen the wrong people to get involved with or makes the same mistakes about relationships over and over again, then the Safe People book offers to walk you through frank, soul-searching questions into active changes and practical steps for growth. http://store.cloudtownsend.com/

The Emotionally Destructive Marriage: How to Find Your Voice and Reclaim Hope - Author Leslie Vernick walks you through steps to assist in safely escaping physical, sexual, emotional, and mental domestic violence. Personal stories of clients she worked with give insight to the realities of this very real issue in many homes.

The Wounded Heart: Hope and Healing for Adult Victims of Childhood Sexual Abuse - Book and Workbook by Author Dr Dan Allender. www.amazon.com

Parents of Children:

American Association of Christian Counselors - Provides referrals for Christian Counselors based on your location. Books and other materials are available. Website www.aacc.net - phone: 1 800-526-8673

Focus on the Family - Provides referrals for Christian Counselors based on your location. Books, conferences and other materials for building healthy relationships are available. Website: www. focusonthefamily.com - phone: 1-800-A-Family

Intentional Parenting: author Linda Stahnke - choosing your path, planning what to train into your child, and how to go about it. Choosing to set yourself and your children up for success as adults and believers in Christ. www.intentionalparenting.org

Living Hope Ministries - Founder/Director TaJuana Davis, Licensed Social Worker/ Professional Christian Life Coach/Family Advocate. Provides support in areas of counsel and coaching. Pastoral Counsel and Family Advocate support for Parenting issues, Crisis Pregnancies, Marriage/Domestic Violence, and tools for strengthening and building stronger coping skills in family relationships. Website: www.livinghopeministriesky.com and www.womenspeakers.com (select KY) - phone: 1 (270) 625-5926.

Raising Great Kids: A Comprehensive Guide to Parenting with Grace and Truth: by Dr. Henry Cloud and Dr. John Townsend - raising children with character that can withstand life's rigors and make the most of its potential. It speaks the language moms and dads speak - it makes sense! http://store.cloudtownsend.com/

Shame Free Parenting: author Sandra D. Wilson shows parents how to regain for themselves a sense of value and purpose--and then how to give those precious gifts to their children and grandchildren.

Too often, being raised in a dysfunctional family environment where healthy nurturing isn't the norm can result in chronic shame later in the adult years. This emotional scarring can leave us desiring joy in life, but seldom grasping it. Wilson illuminates biblical principles to lead adults out of the emotional maze and help parents avoid passing it on to their kids - www.Christian.books.com/

Teens/Parents of Teens:

CJ and Shelley Hitz; Author and Speakers - books that relate to issues teens struggle with daily. For information on conferences and books that include: *Forgiveness Formula; Fuel for the Soul; Mirror, Mirror Am I Beautiful; Unshackled and Free; and True Stories of Forgiveness* call 1-800-230-4390 or email: cj@cjhitz.com or shelley@shelleyhitz.com; website: www.christianspeakers.tv/

Dealing With Today's Teens - offers the parents of teens and pre-teens a new and sometimes shocking glimpse into today's teen culture. Presenter and teacher Mark Gregston offers proven tactics for dealing with difficult teens. He helps parents maintain an open, loving and honest relationship with their teenager. You, too, can learn the key principles and tactics utilized daily by the experts at Heartlight that help troubled teens come to their senses http://www.heartlightministries.org/resources/

Living Hope Ministries - Founder/Director TaJuana Davis, Licensed Social Worker/ Professional Christian Life Coach/Family Advocate. Provides support in areas of counsel and coaching. Pastoral Counsel and Family Advocate support for Parenting issues, Crisis Pregnancies, Marriage/Domestic Violence, and tools for strengthening and building stronger coping skills in family relationships. Website: www.livinghopeministriesky.com and www.womenspeakers.com (select KY) - phone: 1 (270) 625-5926.

Mercy Ministries - Committed to providing the young women we serve, ages 13-28, with excellent program services that allow them to recognize their self-worth and prepare them to reach their full potential. Through the application of God's unconditional love, our approach to healing allows young women to permanently stop destructive cycles and prepares them to take hope out into their communities. **Corporate Office:** PO Box 111060 Nashville, TN 37222-1060 USA **Tel:** 1-(615)-831-6987 **General Fax:** 1-(615)-315-9749 **Admissions Fax:** 1-(615)-831-9953 **Email us at** info@mercyministries.com. Other centers are located in Canada, UK and New Zealand.

Shame Free Parenting: Shame Free Parenting: author Sandra D. Wilson shows parents how to regain for themselves a sense of value and purpose--and then how to give those precious gifts to their children and grandchildren. Too often, being raised in a dysfunctional family environment where healthy nurturing isn't the norm can result in chronic shame later in the adult years. This emotional scarring can leave us desiring joy in life, but seldom grasping it. Wilson illuminates biblical principles to lead adults out of the emotional maze and help parents avoid passing it on to their kids - www.Christianbooks.com.

Teen Challenge USA - By applying biblical principles, Teen Challenge endeavors to help people become mentally-sound, emotionally-balanced, socially-adjusted, physically-well, and spiritually-alive. Goals are to provide youth, adults and families with an effective and comprehensive Christian faith-based solution to life-controlling drug and alcohol problems in order to become productive members of society website: www.teenchallengeusa.com/about/contact - phone: 1 (417) 581-2181

*note (teen challenge is not solely for teens and have locations available throughout the US and internationally for any age, male or female.)

Marriages and Family Relationships:

American Association of Christian Counselors - Provides referrals for Christian Counselors based on your location. Books and other materials are available. Website www.aacc.net - phone: 1 800-526-8673

Before A Bad Goodbye: By Dr. Tim Clinton. For couples at the breaking point, there is a third choice outside of divorce or a marriage in name only: reconciliation. If you're trying to reclaim a love that has nearly slipped through your fingers, you can't afford to miss this outstanding book. Just think about it for a moment: Put two sinners together under one roof and tell them to live happily ever after. Sound impossible? It is, unless God is the foundation. In Before a Bad Goodbye, Dr. Tim Clinton teaches us how to build that foundation one brick at a time. This is a must-read for a divorce-minded culture.

Boundaries in Marriage - Authors Henry Cloud and John Townsend helps you to understand the friction points or serious hurts and betrayals in your marriage--and move beyond them with mutual care, respect, affirmation, and intimacy you both long for http://store.cloudtownsend.com/

Focus on the Family - Provides referrals for Christian Counselors based on your location. Books, conferences and other materials for building healthy relationships are available. Website www.focusonthefamily.com - phone: 1-800-A-Family

Love and Respect - Founder Dr. Emerson and Sarah Eggerichs. Providing conferences and resource materials for married, divorced, separated, dating and single. Men and women will learn how to resolve conflict, dealing with the negative reactions (the crazy cycle). They will also learn how to motivate each other by meeting each other's need (the energizing cycle). Even those who feel hopeless in their relationships will gain understanding on how to handle an indifferent or unresponsive partner (the rewarded cycle) Love and Respect Ministries Inc.770 Kenmoor Ave SE, Ste. #101 Grand Rapids, MI 49546 - phone: 1 (616) 949-9790 www.loveandrespect.com

Renewal Ministries - Founder/Director, George Stahnke. Hope and Healing Through Christ-Centered Ministry for individuals, premarital issues, marriages, relationships, infidelity, homosexuality, spiritual/ministry issues, and pastoral families, 4585 Hilton Parkway, Suite 202 . Colorado Springs CO 80907. Phone: 1 (719) 287-8023 www.renewalcs.org

Pastoral Families:

Care for Pastors - President and Founder Ron and Rodetta Cook - A ministry of encouragement for pastors and wives in helping them know they are worthy of their calling and helping them through counseling, encouragement and temporary housing for small get-away for them. Care for Pastors, 25900 Hwy 27 S Leesburg, FL 34748 - phone: 1(352)728-8179 www.careforpastors.org

En Gedi Retreat - a place of refuge, fun, and relaxation for those who might not otherwise be able to take a vacation. It will serve as one of many things that encourages those that work for the kingdom to continue running the race for the King. Contact us in Yampa, Colorado at www.engediretreat@earthlink.net - phone: 1 (719) 963-3983.

Focus on the Family's 'Thriving Pastor' - provides brotherly encouragement, suggested resources, and a variety of ministry tools for pastors, pastor's wives and pastoral families call us toll-free at 1-800-A-FAMILY - www.thrivingpastor.org

Renewal Ministries - Founder/Director, George Stahnke.- Hope and Healing Through Christ-Centered Ministry for individuals, premarital issues, marriages, relationships, infidelity, homosexuality, spiritual/ministry issues, and pastoral families, 4585 Hilton Parkway, Suite 202 . Colorado Springs CO 80907 - phone: 1 (719) 287-8023 -www.renewalcs.org

Servant Care - Ministry families come to us from all areas of the world, some needing quiet rest, some needing healing from wounds of conflict and persecution, others simply needing to be heard, understood and supported in their time of trials. Whatever the needs, we seek to always be instruments of refreshment and restoration - www.servantcare.com

www.ingramcontent.com/pod-product-compliance
Lightning Source LLC
Chambersburg PA
CBHW030443290526
45786CB00001B/428